February 10, 2010

MEMBERS OF CONGRESS:

I am pleased to forward with this letter the annual report on the multi-agency National Nanotechnology Initiative (NNI). This Supplement to the President's Budget for Fiscal Year 2011 briefly describes the programs and coordinated activities taking place across all 25 of the agencies that are participating today in the NNI. Nanotechnology research and development (R&D) is inherently multidisciplinary and the rate of progress depends on the strong interagency communication, coordination, and collaboration via the National Science and Technology Council to leverage expertise throughout the Federal Government.

The proposed NNI budget for Fiscal Year (FY) 2011 of $1.76 billion will bring the cumulative investment since the inception of the NNI in FY 2001 to nearly $14 billion. This increased investment serves to advance our understanding of nanoscale phenomena and our ability to engineer nanoscale devices and systems that address national priorities and global challenges in such areas as energy conversion and storage, and medicine. At the same time, the NNI investment continues supporting the fundamental, groundbreaking R&D that is the wellspring of U.S. innovation.

Along with its investment in the development and application of nanotechnology, the NNI continues to expand its activities to assess and address the potential health and environmental implications as well as societal and ethical concerns associated with these emerging technologies. The record budget request for direct nanotechnology-related EHS research is consistent with the NNI strategy and represents the agency-level commitment towards implementation, filling gaps and strengthening the fundamental knowledge base for risk-benefit assessment.

The NNI has been widely recognized as a leading model of interagency coordination and collaboration. Nevertheless, the signature initiatives described in the supplement represent the agency efforts to drive more intensive and functional programmatic collaboration where such engagement is essential to meet specific targets in nanotechnology for solar energy, electronics, and sustainable nanomanufacturing.

Nanotechnology R&D constitutes a core building block of innovation that will ultimately accelerate job creation and transform many sectors of our economy through commercialization. The NNI reflects a longstanding commitment to broad-based support of closely-integrated applications and implications research to enable nanotechnology innovation in the United States that continues to set the pace for the rest of the world.

Sincerely,

John P. Holdren
Director

About the National Science and Technology Council

The National Science and Technology Council (NSTC) was established by Executive Order on November 23, 1993. The Cabinet-level council is the principal means by which the President coordinates science, space, and technology policies across the Federal Government. NSTC coordinates the diverse parts of the Federal research and development enterprise. An important objective of the NSTC is the establishment of clear national goals for Federal science and technology investments in areas ranging from nanotechnology and health research to improving transportation systems and strengthening fundamental research. The Council prepares research and development strategies that are coordinated across Federal agencies to form a comprehensive investment package aimed at accomplishing multiple national goals. To obtain additional information regarding the NSTC, visit the NSTC website at http://www.ostp.gov/cs/nstc.

About the Office of Science and Technology Policy

The Office of Science and Technology Policy (OSTP) was established by the National Science and Technology Policy, Organization, and Priorities Act of 1976. OSTP's responsibilities include advising the President in policy formulation and budget development on all questions in which science and technology (S&T) are important elements; articulating the President's S&T policies and programs; and fostering strong partnerships among Federal, state, and local governments, and the scientific communities in industry and academia. The Director of OSTP also serves as Assistant to the President for Science and Technology and manages the NSTC for the President. For additional information regarding OSTP, visit the OSTP website at http://www.ostp.gov/.

About this document

This document is a supplement to the President's 2011 Budget Request submitted to Congress on February 1, 2010. It gives a description of the activities underway in 2010 and planned for 2011 by the Federal Government agencies participating in the National Nanotechnology Initiative (NNI), primarily from a programmatic and budgetary perspective. It is based on the NNI Strategic Plan released in December 2007 and reports estimated investments for 2010 and requested investments for 2011 by program component area (PCA), as called for under the provisions of the 21st Century Nanotechnology Research and Development Act (Public Law 108-153). Additional information regarding the NNI is available on the NNI website at http://www.nano.gov/.

About the cover

Central image: A dark field optical microscope image of breast cancer cells with gold nanopyramids attached to the cell surfaces by antibodies on the nanopyramids. Because of the targeting provided by the antibodies, the gold nanoparticles can be used as both localized therapeutic agents and diagnostic probes. The pyramids are about 200 nanometers at their base and taper to about 1 nanometer at their tips. In the image shown, the gold nanopyramids appear as bright orange spots. The cells are about 10 micrometers in diameter. The nanoparticles can behave as high contrast probes to identify cancer cells and to visualize the location of biomarkers. When illuminated with near-infrared light, the nanopyramids generate heat that can be used to locally destroy cancer cells without harming the surrounding healthy cells. The ultra-sharp tip and edges of the nanopyramids produce highly concentrated electromagnetic fields that can further enhance their heating abilities (work funded by NIH NCI Alliance for Nanotechnology in Cancer and NIH Director's Pioneer Award; courtesy of Teri W. Odom, Northwestern University, http://chemgroups.northwestern.edu/odom/ and Thomas V. O'Halloran, Northwestern University, http://chemgroups.northwestern.edu/ohalloran/).

Background image: False-color scanning electron microscopy image of the gold nanopyramids situated on silicon pedestals as they are formed using high-resolution lithography; the spacing of the pedestals is about two micrometers. This image demonstrates how anisotropic particles made by nanofabrication methods are highly uniform in size and can be three-dimensional in shape. The method also enables selective functionalization of the nanoparticle surfaces (work funded by NSF; courtesy of Teri W. Odom).

Cover and book design

Cover design is by N. R. Sayo-Art LLC. Book design is by staff members of the National Nanotechnology Coordination Office (NNCO).

Copyright information

Printed in the United States of America. 2010.

Report prepared by
NATIONAL SCIENCE AND TECHNOLOGY COUNCIL
COMMITTEE ON TECHNOLOGY (CT)
SUBCOMMITTEE ON NANOSCALE SCIENCE, ENGINEERING, AND TECHNOLOGY (NSET)

CT Co-Chairs: Aneesh Chopra, Office of Science and Technology Policy
                         Vivek Kundra, Office of Management and Budget

CT Executive Secretary: Jason E. Boehm, National Institute of Standards and Technology

NSET Subcommittee Agency Co-Chair: National Nanotechnology Coordination Office Director:
  Sally S. Tinkle   E. Clayton Teague

NSET Subcommittee OSTP Co-Chair: NSET Subcommittee Executive Secretary:
  Travis M. Earles   Geoffrey M. Holdridge

Department and Agency Representatives

Office of Science and Technology Policy (OSTP)
  Travis M. Earles

Office of Management and Budget (OMB)
  Irene B. Kariampuzha

Bureau of Industry and Security (BIS/DOC)
  Kelly Gardner

Consumer Product Safety Commission (CPSC)
  Mary Ann Danello
  Treye A. Thomas

National Institute of Food and Agriculture (NIFA/USDA)
  Hongda Chen

Department of Defense (DOD)
  Lewis Sloter
  Mihal E. Gross
  Gernot S. Pomrenke
  Eric Snow
  David M. Stepp

Department of Education (DOEd)
  Krishan Mathur

Department of Energy (DOE)
  Patricia M. Dehmer
  Altaf H. Carim
  Chien-Wei Li
  John C. Miller
  Andrew R. Schwartz
  Brian G. Valentine

Department of Homeland Security (DHS)
  Richard T. Lareau
  Eric J. Houser

Department of Justice (DOJ)
  Joseph Heaps

Department of Labor (DOL)
  Brad Wiggins

Department of State (DOS)
  Ken Hodgkins
  Chris Cannizzaro

Department of Transportation (DOT)
  Kelly Leone
  Jonathan R. Porter

Department of the Treasury (DOTreas)
  John F. Bobalek

Director of National Intelligence (DNI)
  Richard Ridgley
  Susan E. Durham

Environmental Protection Agency (EPA)
  Jeff Morris
  Nora F. Savage
  Philip G. Sayre

Food and Drug Administration (FDA/DHHS)
  Jesse Goodman
  Carlos Peña

Forest Service (FS/USDA)
  Christopher D. Risbrudt
  Theodore H. Wegner

International Trade Commission (ITC)
  Elizabeth R. Nesbitt

National Aeronautics and Space Administration (NASA)
  Minoo N. Dastoor

National Institute for Occupational Safety and Health (NIOSH/CDC/DHHS)
  Charles L. Geraci
  Vladimir V. Murashov

National Institutes of Health (NIH/DHHS)
  Piotr Grodzinski
  Lori Henderson
  Jeffery A. Schloss

National Institute of Standards and Technology (NIST/DOC)
  Lloyd J. Whitman

National Science Foundation (NSF)
  Mihail C. Roco
  Zakya H. Kafafi
  Parag R. Chitnis
  T. James Rudd

Nuclear Regulatory Commission (NRC)
  Richard P. Croteau

U.S. Geological Survey (USGS)
  Sarah Gerould

U.S. Patent and Trademark Office (USPTO/DOC)
  Charles Eloshway
  Bruce Kisliuk

TABLE OF CONTENTS

1. INTRODUCTION AND OVERVIEW

Overview of the National Nanotechnology Initiative

The National Nanotechnology Initiative (NNI) is a U.S. Government research and development (R&D) program of twenty-five agencies working together toward the common challenging vision of *"a future in which the ability to understand and control matter at the nanoscale leads to a revolution in technology and industry that benefits society."* The combined, coordinated efforts of these agencies have accelerated discovery, development, and deployment of nanotechnology towards agency missions and the broader national interest. Established in 2001,[1] the NNI involves nanotechnology-related activities by the 25 agencies shown in Table 1, 15 of which have budgets for nanotechnology R&D for 2011.

The National Nanotechnology Initiative is managed within the framework of the National Science and Technology Council (NSTC), the Cabinet-level council by which the President coordinates science and technology policy across the Federal Government. The Nanoscale Science, Engineering, and Technology (NSET) Subcommittee of the NSTC coordinates planning, budgeting, program implementation, and review of the initiative. The NSET Subcommittee is composed of representatives from agencies participating in the NNI. A listing of official NSET Subcommittee members is provided at the front of this report. Contact information for NSET Subcommittee participants is provided in Appendix B. The National Nanotechnology Coordination Office (NNCO) acts as the primary point of contact for information on the NNI; provides technical and administrative support to the NSET Subcommittee; supports the subcommittee in the preparation of multiagency planning, budget, and assessment documents, including this report; develops, updates, and maintains the NNI website (http://www.nano.gov); and provides public outreach on behalf of the NNI.

The NSET Subcommittee has established four working groups: (1) the Global Issues in Nanotechnology (GIN) Working Group, (2) the Nanotechnology Environmental and Health Implications (NEHI) Working Group, (3) the Nanomanufacturing, Industry Liaison, and Innovation (NILI) Working Group, and (4) the Nanotechnology Public Engagement and Communication (NPEC) Working Group.

The December 2007 NNI Strategic Plan[2] sets out the vision for the NNI stated above. The plan specifies four goals aimed at achieving that overall vision: (1) advance a world-class nanotechnology research and development program; (2) foster the transfer of new technologies into products for commercial and public

---

What is Nanotechnology?

Nanotechnology is the understanding and control of matter at dimensions between approximately 1 and 100 nanometers, where unique phenomena enable novel applications. Encompassing nanoscale science, engineering, and technology, nanotechnology involves imaging, measuring, modeling, and manipulating matter at this length scale.

A nanometer is one-billionth of a meter. A sheet of paper is about 100,000 nanometers thick; a single gold atom is about a third of a nanometer in diameter. Dimensions between approximately 1 and 100 nanometers are known as the nanoscale. Unusual physical, chemical, and biological properties can emerge in materials at the nanoscale. These properties may differ in important ways from the properties of bulk materials and single atoms or molecules.

---

[1] **General note:** In conformance with Office of Management and Budget style, references to years in this report are to fiscal years unless otherwise noted.

[2] http://www.nano.gov/NNI_Strategic_Plan_2007.pdf. Note that this plan will be updated in 2010.

benefit; (3) develop and sustain educational resources, a skilled workforce, and the supporting infrastructure and tools to advance nanotechnology; and (4) support responsible development of nanotechnology. The plan also lays out eight NNI investment categories (or program component areas, PCAs), each aimed at helping to achieve one or more of the above goals:

1. Fundamental nanoscale phenomena and processes

2. Nanomaterials

3. Nanoscale devices and systems

4. Instrumentation research, metrology, and standards for nanotechnology

5. Nanomanufacturing

6. Major research facilities and instrumentation acquisition

7. Environment, health, and safety

8. Education and societal dimensions

Federal agencies are investing in R&D within the above categories in support of national goals and agency missions. NNI funding represents the sum of the nanotechnology-related funding allocated by each of the participating agencies. Each agency separately determines its budgets for nanotechnology R&D, in coordination with the Office of Management and Budget, the Office of Science and Technology Policy, and Congress. Thus, the NNI is an interagency budget crosscut in which participating agencies work closely with each other to create an integrated program through communication, coordination, and collaboration. Enhanced communications through committee and working groups has led to joint coordination and collaboration in a variety of forms, including sharing of knowledge and expertise; joint sponsorship of solicitations and workshops; and leveraging funding, staff, and facility/equipment resources at NNI participating agencies. Examples of focused R&D collaboration across agencies include the Nanotechnology Signature Initiatives summarized in the sidebar on page 6.

Purpose of this Report

This document provides supplemental information to the President's 2011 Budget and serves as the Annual Report on the NNI called for in the 21st Century Nanotechnology Research and Development Act (P.L. 108-153, 15 USC 7501). In particular, the report summarizes NNI programmatic activities for 2009 and 2010, as well as those planned for in 2011. This report also meets the requirements for the Department of Defense of 10 USC 2358 "Research and Development Projects" as amended by the National Defense Authorization Act for 2010 (H.R. 2647). NNI budgets for 2009–2011 are presented by agency and PCA in Section 2 of this report. Information on the use of the Small Business Innovation Research (SBIR) and Small Business Technology Transfer (STTR) program funds to support nanotechnology research and commercialization activities, also called for in P.L. 108-153, is included at the end of Section 2. Section 3 summarizes the perspectives of the NNI agencies regarding their nanotechnology investments. Section 4 highlights activities that have been undertaken and progress that has been made toward achieving the goals set out in the NNI Strategic Plan and discusses external reviews of the NNI and how their recommendations are being addressed.

Table 1
List of Federal Agencies Participating in the NNI During 2010

Federal agencies with budgets dedicated to nanotechnology research and development

Consumer Product Safety Commission (CPSC)
Department of Defense (DOD)
Department of Energy (DOE)
Department of Homeland Security (DHS)
Department of Justice (DOJ)
Department of Transportation (DOT, including the Federal Highway Administration, FHWA)
Environmental Protection Agency (EPA)
Food and Drug Administration (FDA, Department of Health and Human Services)
Forest Service (FS, Department of Agriculture)
National Aeronautics and Space Administration (NASA)
National Institute for Occupational Safety and Health (NIOSH, Department of Health and Human Services/Centers for Disease Control and Prevention)
National Institute of Food and Agriculture (NIFA, Department of Agriculture)[3]
National Institutes of Health (NIH, Department of Health and Human Services)
National Institute of Standards and Technology (NIST, Department of Commerce)
National Science Foundation (NSF)

Other participating agencies

Bureau of Industry and Security (BIS, Department of Commerce)
Department of Education (DOEd)
Department of Labor (DOL)
Department of State (DOS)
Department of the Treasury (DOTreas)
Director of National Intelligence (DNI)
International Trade Commission (ITC)
Nuclear Regulatory Commission (NRC)
U.S. Geological Survey (USGS, Department of the Interior)
U.S. Patent and Trademark Office (USPTO, Department of Commerce)

[3] Section 7511 of the Food, Conservation, and Energy Act of 2008 (FCEA) established within the Department of Agriculture the National Institute of Food and Agriculture (NIFA) and transferred all authorities of the Cooperative State Research, Education, and Extension Service (CSREES) to NIFA not later than October 1, 2009.

Nanotechnology Signature Initiatives

To accelerate nanotechnology development in support of the President's priorities and innovation strategy, NNI member agencies have identified areas ripe for significant advances through close and targeted program-level interagency collaboration. The resulting Nanotechnology Signature Initiatives for 2011 are summarized as follows (details are available at http://www.nano.gov/html/research/signature_initiatives.html):

Nanotechnology Applications for Solar Energy (DOE, NIST, NSF, DOD, DNI, USDA/NIFA – $51 million total)*

The President's Agenda calls for the development of carbon-neutral alternative energy sources to mitigate global climate change, reduce dependence on foreign oil, improve the economy, and improve the environment. The specific targets specified by the President's Agenda state that 10 percent of electricity generated should be derived from renewable sources by 2012 and 25 percent by 2025.

Solar energy is a promising alternative energy source that can address these challenges. It is readily available, free from geopolitical tension and not a threat to the environment through pollution or to the climate through greenhouse gas emission. The development of a solar energy infrastructure will not only support U.S. energy independence, but also represents an unparalleled economic opportunity if the U.S. can maintain scientific and industrial leadership in this field.

Today, the current rate of improvement of solar technology performance is inadequate to meet future energy needs, and the cost is often not economically competitive without subsidies. Therefore, new innovations and fundamental breakthroughs are needed to accelerate the development of economical solar energy technologies that overcome the limits of existing technologies.

Nanotechnology provides a key to overcoming current performance barriers and substantially improving the collection and conversion of solar energy. At the nanoscale, a number of physical phenomena have been identified that can improve the collection and conversion of solar energy. Nanoparticles and nanostructures have been shown to enhance the absorption of light, increase the conversion of light to electricity, and provide better thermal storage and transport. However, current demonstrations of these technologies fall short of potential performance because of poor control over feature size and placement, unpredictable micro/nanostructure, and poor interface formation. The goal of this initiative is to exploit the benefits of nanotechnology by enhancing understanding of conversion and storage phenomena at the nanoscale, improving nanoscale characterization of electronic properties, and helping enable economical nanomanufacturing.

Sustainable Nanomanufacturing (NIST, NSF, DOE, EPA, NIH – $23 million total)*

A long-term vision for nanomanufacturing is to create flexible, "bottom-up" batch assembly methods that can be used to assemble elaborate systems of complex nanodevices. To create the foundation for achieving this vision, over the next decade the goal of this initiative is to accelerate the development of industrial-scale methods for manufacturing of functional systems with relatively limited complexity based on manufactured nanoparticles with designed properties. The organized assemblies of nanoparticles manufactured will be designed to control and manipulate information, thermal energy, and electromagnetic radiation. The systems to be manufactured, based on these methods, will include disruptive technologies for high-speed communication and computation, solar energy harvesting, waste heat management and recovery, and energy storage. If the initiative is successful, the methods developed will be immediately extendable to more complex components and systems as future nanodevices mature.

Nanoelectronics for 2020 and Beyond (NSF, DOD, NIST, DOE, DNI – $55 million total)*

Continuing to shrink the dimensions of electronic devices is important in order to further increase processing speed, reduce device switching energy, increase system functionality, and reduce manufacturing cost per bit. But as the dimensions of critical elements of devices approach atomic size, quantum tunneling and other quantum effects degrade and ultimately prohibit conventional device operation. Researchers are therefore pursuing somewhat radical approaches to overcome these fundamental physics limitations. Candidate approaches include different types of logic using cellular automata or quantum entanglement and superposition; 3-D spatial architectures; and information-carrying variables other than electron charge, such as photon polarization, electron spin, and position and states of atoms and molecules. Approaches based on nanoscale science, engineering, and technology are the most promising for realizing these radical changes and are expected to change the very nature of electronics and the essence of how electronic devices are manufactured. Rapidly reinforcing domestic R&D successes in these arenas could establish a U.S. domestic manufacturing base that will dominate 21st-century electronics commerce. The goal of this initiative is to accelerate the discovery and use of novel nanoscale fabrication processes and innovative concepts to produce revolutionary materials, devices, systems, and architectures to advance the field of nanoelectronics.

These Nanotechnology Signature Initiatives represent the leading edge of functional interagency collaboration in the budget and program planning process under the NNI, with multiple agencies working in common toward specific objectives.

* Funding commitments by participating agencies at the time this supplement was completed are listed above. Updated/new commitments will be provided at http://www.nano.gov/html/research/signature_initiatives.html.

2. NNI INVESTMENTS

Budget Summary

The 2011 Budget provides nearly $1.8 billion for the National Nanotechnology Initiative (NNI), reflecting continued steady growth in the NNI investment. This sustained major investment in nanotechnology research and development (R&D) across the Federal Government over the past eleven years of the NNI, spanning three Presidential Administrations and five Congresses, is an indication of the broad support for this program. This support is based on nanotechnology's potential to vastly improve our fundamental understanding and control of matter at the nanoscale, ultimately leading to a revolution in technology and industry for the benefit of society. While the NNI remains focused on fulfilling the Federal role of supporting basic research, infrastructure development, and technology transfer, the proposed investments for 2011 place renewed emphasis on accelerating the transition from basic R&D advances and capabilities into innovations that support national priorities such as sustainable energy technologies, healthcare, and environmental protection. This is consistent with substantial increases in the requested nanotechnology investments for 2011 at the Department of Energy, the National Institutes of Health, and the Environmental Protection Agency. The NNI is also increasing its investments aimed at implementing the Government's strategy for nanotechnology-related environmental, health, and safety (EHS) research.[4] As a part of this expanded EHS effort, the Food and Drug Administration and the Consumer Product Safety Commission are participating in the formal NNI budget crosscut for the first time in 2011. Increasing investments in nanotechnology R&D by other NNI participating agencies reflect the potential for this research to support diverse agency missions and responsibilities. The cumulative NNI investment since 2001, including the 2011 request, now totals over $14 billion. This includes $511 million in funding authorized under the American Recovery and Reinvestment Act of 2009 (P.L. 111-5). Cumulative investments in EHS research since 2005 now total over $480 million. Cumulative investments in education and in research on ethical, legal, and other societal dimensions of nanotechnology since 2005 total over $260 million.

The 2011 NNI budget supports nanoscale science, engineering, and technology R&D at 15 agencies. Agencies with the largest investments are:

- DOE (research providing a basis for new and improved energy technologies)
- NSF (fundamental research across all disciplines of science and engineering)
- NIH (nanotechnology-based biomedical research at the intersection of life sciences and the physical sciences)
- DOD (science and engineering research advancing defense and dual-use capabilities)
- NIST (fundamental research and development of measurement and fabrication tools, analytical methodologies, and metrology for nanotechnology)

Other agencies investing in mission-related research are EPA, NIOSH, NASA, FDA, DHS, USDA (including both NIFA and FS), CPSC, DOT (including FHWA), and DOJ.

Table 2 shows NNI investments in 2009–2011 for Federal agencies with budgets and investments for nanotechnology R&D. Tables 3–6 list the investments for 2009–2011 by agency and by program component area (PCA).

---

[4] *Strategy for Nanotechnology-Related Environmental, Health, and Safety Research* (February 2008): http://www.nano.gov/NNI_EHS_Research_Strategy.pdf. NNI EHS research is defined as research whose primary purpose is to understand and address potential risks to health and the environment that engineered nanomaterials may pose.

Table 2: NNI Budget, by Agency, 2009–2011 (dollars in millions)				
Agency	2009 Actual	2009 Recovery*	2010 Estimated	2011 Proposed
DOE**	332.6	293.2	372.9	423.9
NSF	408.6	101.2	417.7	401.3
HHS/NIH	342.8	73.4	360.6	382.4
DOD***	459.0	0.0	436.4	348.5
DOC/NIST	93.4	43.4	114.4	108.0
EPA	11.6	0.0	17.7	20.0
HHS/NIOSH	6.7	0.0	9.5	16.5
NASA	13.7	0.0	13.7	15.8
HHS/FDA	6.5	0.0	7.3	15.0
DHS	9.1	0.0	11.7	11.7
USDA/NIFA	9.9	0.0	10.4	8.9
USDA/FS	5.4	0.0	5.4	5.4
CPSC	0.2	0.0	0.2	2.2
DOT/FHWA	0.9	0.0	3.2	2.0
DOJ	1.2	0.0	0.0	0.0
TOTAL****	**1,701.5**	**511.3**	**1,781.1**	**1,761.6**

*   Based on allocations of the American Recovery and Reinvestment Act of 2009 (P.L. 111-5) appropriations. Agencies may report additional ARRA funding for SBIR and STTR projects later, when 2009 SBIR/STTR data become available.

**   Funding levels for DOE include the Office of Science, the Office of Energy Efficiency and Renewable Energy, the Office of Fossil Energy, the Office of Nuclear Energy, and the Advanced Research Projects Agency–Energy.

***   In Tables 2–4, the 2009 and 2010 DOD figures include Congressionally directed funding that is outside the NNI plan ($117 million for 2009).

****   For Tables 2–7, totals may not add, due to rounding.

Key points about the 2010 and 2011 NNI investments

- Beyond the $1.7 billion in total NNI investments reported under the respective 2009 agency appropriations, an additional $511 million was provided for nanotechnology research and infrastructure investments in 2009 through the American Recovery and Reinvestment Act (ARRA) of 2009. This substantial ARRA enhancement to the NNI in 2009 included investments across all of the NNI PCAs, with particular emphasis on PCA 2 (nanomaterials, where DOE alone increased its investment by $138 million) and on PCA 6 (major research facilities & instrumentation acquisition), where NIST, DOE, and NSF allocated over $72 million to upgrade equipment and facilities at NNI user facilities and research centers.

- Research on fundamental nanoscale phenomena and processes (PCA 1) remains the largest program component area, with $484 million requested for 2011. Combined with PCA 2 (nanomaterials, $342 million in the 2011 request), this basic research component of the NNI portfolio represents just under half of the total NNI funding request, reflecting the continued importance of sustained Federal funding for fundamental research, feeding the innovation pipeline.

- The Department of Energy now has the largest nanotechnology investment among the NNI agencies, requesting a total of $424 million for 2011. The increase in 2011 over 2010 is due in part to new investments at the Advanced Research Projects Agency–Energy (ARPA–E), as well as increased funding at the Office of Science and the Office of Energy Efficiency and Renewable Energy.

Table 3: Actual 2009 Agency Investments by Program Component Area (dollars in millions)								
	1. Fundamental Phenomena & Processes	2. Nanomaterials	3. Nanoscale Devices & Systems	4. Instrument Research, Metrology, & Standards	5. Nano-manufacturing	6. Major Research Facilities & Instr. Acquisition	7. Environment, Health, and Safety	8. Education & Societal Dimensions	NNI Total
DOE	99.8	92.8	7.9	21.1	6.9	100.5	3.1	0.5	332.6
NSF	143.6	72.4	54.0	21.4	27.7	31.5	26.8	31.3	408.6
HHS/NIH	46.7	73.9	172.4	17.5	2.2	13.6	12.0	4.5	342.8
DOD	162.8	67.5	166.9	9.0	29.0	19.7	4.1	0.0	459.0
DOC/NIST	23.1	8.5	17.0	19.4	9.4	12.4	3.5	0.0	93.4
EPA	0.2	0.2	0.1	0.0	0.0	0.0	11.1	0.0	11.6
HHS/NIOSH	0.0	0.0	0.0	0.0	0.0	0.0	6.7	0.0	6.7
NASA	0.0	8.6	5.1	0.0	0.0	0.0	0.0	0.0	13.7
HHS/FDA	0.0	0.0	0.0	0.0	0.0	0.0	6.5	0.0	6.5
DHS	0.0	3.7	5.3	0.0	0.1	0.0	0.0	0.0	9.1
USDA/NIFA	1.0	2.0	5.7	0.0	0.2	0.0	0.5	0.5	9.9
USDA/FS	2.0	1.4	0.7	1.1	0.2	0.0	0.0	0.0	5.4
CPSC	0.0	0.0	0.0	0.0	0.0	0.0	0.2	0.0	0.2
DOT/FHWA	0.0	0.9	0.0	0.0	0.0	0.0	0.0	0.0	0.9
DOJ	0.0	0.0	0.0	1.2	0.0	0.0	0.0	0.0	1.2
TOTAL	479.2	331.9	435.2	90.8	75.6	177.6	74.5	36.8	1701.5

Table 4: 2009 Agency Investments from the ARRA by Program Component Area (dollars in millions)								
	1. Fundamental Phenomena & Processes	2. Nanomaterials	3. Nanoscale Devices & Systems	4. Instrument Research, Metrology, & Standards	5. Nano-manufacturing	6. Major Research Facilities & Instr. Acquisition	7. Environment, Health, and Safety	8. Education & Societal Dimensions	NNI Total
DOE	85.9	137.9	21.8	3.5	18.9	25.0	0.2	0.0	293.2
NSF	29.9	24.7	17.6	4.5	6.1	6.5	3.4	8.5	101.2
HHS/NIH	14.7	15.7	28.6	4.4	0.4	0.7	8.4	0.5	73.4
DOC/NIST	0.0	0.0	0.0	0.0	3.1	40.3	0.0	0.0	43.4
TOTAL	130.6	178.3	68.0	12.4	28.5	72.5	12.0	9.0	511.3

- While funding for PCAs 1 and 2 has been sustained, the fastest-growing PCAs in recent years have been those for environment, health, and safety (PCA 7, increasing from $35 million in 2005 to $117 million in the 2011 request) and nanomanufacturing (PCA 5, increasing from $34 million in 2006 to $101 million in the 2011 request). This is consistent with the NNI's commitment to the goal of supporting responsible development of nanotechnology, and with broad recognition of the importance of both EHS and manufacturing research to realizing the true potential benefits of nanotechnology.

Table 5: Estimated 2010 Agency Investments by Program Component Area (dollars in millions)								
	1. Fundamental Phenomena & Processes	2. Nanomaterials	3. Nanoscale Devices & Systems	4. Instrument Research, Metrology, & Standards	5. Nano-manufacturing	6. Major Research Facilities & Instr. Acquisition	7. Environment, Health, and Safety	8. Education & Societal Dimensions	NNI Total
DOE	103.0	114.5	17.2	21.8	7.0	106.3	2.6	0.5	372.9
NSF	152.6	78.7	43.7	18.3	22.4	37.8	29.8	34.3	417.7
HHS/NIH	48.0	75.9	180.7	18.0	2.2	14.0	17.3	4.6	360.6
DOD	138.8	75.3	148.0	5.9	37.2	28.0	3.1	0.0	436.4
DOC/NIST	22.3	8.4	22.5	19.1	27.2	11.2	3.6	0.0	114.4
EPA	0.2	0.2	0.2	0.0	0.0	0.0	17.1	0.0	17.7
HHS/NIOSH	0.0	0.0	0.0	0.0	0.0	0.0	9.5	0.0	9.5
NASA	0.0	8.6	5.1	0.0	0.0	0.0	0.0	0.0	13.7
HHS/FDA	0.0	0.0	0.0	0.0	0.0	0.0	7.3	0.0	7.3
DHS	0.0	6.5	4.9	0.0	0.3	0.0	0.0	0.0	11.7
USDA/NIFA	1.0	2.0	5.7	0.0	0.2	0.0	1.0	0.5	10.4
USDA/FS	2.0	1.4	0.7	1.1	0.2	0.0	0.0	0.0	5.4
CPSC	0.0	0.0	0.0	0.0	0.0	0.0	0.2	0.0	0.2
DOT/FHWA	0.0	2.0	1.2	0.0	0.0	0.0	0.0	0.0	3.2
DOJ	0.0	0.0	0.0	0.0	0.0	0.0	0.0	0.0	0.0
TOTAL	467.9	373.5	429.9	84.3	96.7	197.3	91.6	39.9	1781.1

Table 6: Proposed 2011 Agency Investments by Program Component Area (dollars in millions)								
	1. Fundamental Phenomena & Processes	2. Nanomaterials	3. Nanoscale Devices & Systems	4. Instrument Research, Metrology, & Standards	5. Nano-manufacturing	6. Major Research Facilities & Instr. Acquisition	7. Environment, Health, and Safety	8. Education & Societal Dimensions	NNI Total
DOE	117.2	121.7	30.4	19.3	20.9	111.3	2.6	0.5	423.9
NSF	140.1	74.3	40.7	16.6	32.2	35.3	33.0	29.0	401.3
HHS/NIH	50.3	80.0	193.8	18.6	2.3	14.4	18.3	4.7	382.4
DOD	151.5	39.3	99.0	2.5	25.1	30.7	0.5	0.0	348.5
DOC/NIST	22.4	8.2	20.2	18.5	20.2	11.2	7.3	0.0	108.0
EPA	0.2	0.1	0.2	0.0	0.0	0.0	19.5	0.0	20.0
HHS/NIOSH	0.0	0.0	0.0	0.0	0.0	0.0	16.5	0.0	16.5
NASA	0.0	8.4	7.4	0.0	0.0	0.0	0.0	0.0	15.8
HHS/FDA	0.0	0.0	0.0	0.0	0.0	0.0	15.0	0.0	15.0
DHS	0.0	6.5	4.9	0.0	0.3	0.0	0.0	0.0	11.7
USDA/NIFA	0.7	1.4	3.8	0.3	0.2	0.0	2.0	0.5	8.9
USDA/FS	2.0	1.4	0.7	1.1	0.2	0.0	0.0	0.0	5.4
CPSC	0.0	0.0	0.0	0.0	0.0	0.0	2.2	0.0	2.2
DOT/FHWA	0.0	1.0	1.0	0.0	0.0	0.0	0.0	0.0	2.0
DOJ	0.0	0.0	0.0	0.0	0.0	0.0	0.0	0.0	0.0
TOTAL	484.4	342.3	402.0	76.9	101.4	203.0	116.9	34.8	1761.6

- There are significant increases requested in nanomanufacturing for 2011—over $26 million, or about 34%, over 2009. A major component of this increase results from the NIST Technology Innovation Program identifying the practical application of advanced materials as an area of critical national need. These advanced materials include nanomaterials, advanced alloys, and composites in manufacturing, resulting in a new 2010 investment in nanomanufacturing.

- NIH's investments in nanotechnology continue to grow, from $40 million in 2001 to $382 million in the 2011 request, as diagnostic and therapeutic applications show increasing promise and maturity.

- Investments in environmental, health, and safety research continue to grow substantially, from $87 million in 2009 (including $12 million in ARRA funds) to a requested $117 million for 2011. The requested EHS investment for 2011 is over triple the figure for 2005 ($35 million). The increases are primarily targeted for those agencies serving as leading agencies for the five R&D categories identified in the NNI *Strategy for Nanotechnology-Related Environmental, Health, and Safety Research* (http://www.nano.gov/NNI_EHS_Research_Strategy.pdf). Increased funding is provided for some aspects of all five categories of EHS R&D.

- Other leading funding categories include the PCAs on nanoscale devices and systems (PCA 3, $402 million in 2011) and major research facilities and instrumentation acquisition (PCA 6, $203 million in 2011). PCA 3 is growing as nanotechnology R&D moves from passive nanostructures to active devices and complex systems. Sustained investments in the NNI research infrastructure funded under PCA 6, with over 60 centers and user facilities spread across the nation, assure that U.S. researchers and industries have continued access to the world-class facilities and equipment needed to sustain U.S. competitiveness in nanoscale science and technology. Increased funds provided for PCA 6 under ARRA in 2009 were used to upgrade equipment and other facilities at DOE, NSF, and NIST user facilities.

- The largest percentage increases in nanotechnology-related funding for 2011 are at agencies that have had relatively modest nanotechnology investments in the past. Agencies with responsibilities related to EHS issues such as FDA, CPSC, NIOSH, and EPA are requesting significant increases in funding. USDA has also increased its investments in recent years, more than doubling the nanotechnology budget at the National Institute for Food and Agriculture (NIFA, formerly CSREES) since 2007 (from $3.9 million in 2007 to $8.9 million in the 2011 request), and now including a $5.4 million request for nanotechnology R&D at the Forest Service.

Changes in Balance of Investments by Program Component Area (PCA)[5]

P.L. 108-153 calls for this report to address changes in the balance of investments by NNI member agencies among the PCAs. These are summarized below for those agencies that are reporting changes for 2010 and 2011.

DOD: The DOD does not foresee major changes in its overall investment portfolio in the nanotechnology program component areas. With the increasing maturation of nanotechnology research, however, increased investment in the broad area of nanomanufacturing (PCA 5) appears likely. Some examples of areas being emphasized include the following: (1) creation of highly uniform arrays of carbon nanotubes with an electronic grade junction to a silicon semiconductor substrate for ultra-lightweight, uncooled infrared detectors, (2) development of bio-enabled fabrication of electronics that bridges top-down and bottom-up approaches to achieve better than 10-nm spatial resolution, and (3) development of

---

[5] Changes are as compared to NNI investments described in the NNI Supplement to the President's 2010 Budget, http://www.nano.gov/html/res/pubs.html.

electrochemical techniques for patterning metals to produce nanoscale features for antennas, sensors, meta-materials, and catalysts.

DOE: The predominant DOE components of the NNI are research programs and facilities supported by DOE's Office of Science. The investment in 2011 continues to support full operation of the five DOE Nanoscale Science Research Center (NSRC) user facilities (corresponding to PCA 6, major research facilities and instrumentation acquisition) and an extensive array of individual university grants and laboratory research programs. The Energy Frontier Research Centers, larger collaborative efforts in which a portion of the activity relates to nanoscale science, are also continued. In 2010 DOE initiates an Energy Innovation Hub on Fuels from Sunlight, and this support will continue in 2011, with a portion of the activity related to nanoscience. Nanoscience funding increases in 2011 are due partly to small increases across all of these mechanisms, with an emphasis on addressing grand science challenges to achieve atomic and molecular control of matter and energy. However, much of the increase in 2011 over 2010 results from new funding from ARPA-E, the initiation of additional Energy Frontier Research Centers, and the formation of a second Energy Innovation Hub focusing on batteries and energy storage. It is anticipated that a fraction of these activities will be appropriately characterized as nanoscience. The DOE investment in 2011 includes moderate increases across multiple PCAs.

DOT/FHWA: The FHWA's planned increase to its overall nanotechnology investment will be maintained in 2010. 2010 funding will be applied to both nanomaterials (PCA 2) and to nanoscale devices and systems (PCA 3).

CPSC: Formally joining the NNI budget crosscut for the first time in 2011, CPSC is requesting $2 million in increased funding in 2011 in PCA 7 (environment, health, and safety) to allow it to participate with other agencies in researching safety aspects of nanomaterials use in consumer products. Planned 2011 programs include working with other agencies on (1) developing protocols to assess the potential release of airborne nanoparticles from various consumer products and to determine their contributions to human exposure; (2) determining whether nanomaterials can be used for performance improvement in sports safety equipment such as helmets and kneepads without creating other health hazards; (3) expanding consumer product testing using scientifically credible protocols to evaluate the exposure potential from nanosilver in consumer products, with special emphasis on exposures to young children; and (4) working across agencies to assure that shared common public health concerns are met in research studies to determine potential impacts on the public health of nanomaterial use in consumer products.

FDA: Formally joining the National Nanotechnology Initiative budget crosscut for the first time in 2011, FDA will conduct activities in PCA 7 (environment, health, and safety) that support the following agency-wide priorities: (1) laboratory and product testing capacity, (2) scientific staff development and training, and (3) collaborative and interdisciplinary research to address product characterization and safety. Together, these investments will support responsible development of nanotechnology.

NIH: The NIH nanotechnology investment continues to grow (12.5% from 2008 to 2009). Under the American Recovery and Reinvestment Act (ARRA) of 2009 (Public Law 111-5), NIH invested in PCA 7 (environment, health, and safety). In addition to the approximately $13 million that NIH's National Institute of Environmental Health Sciences (NIEHS) invested in nanotechnology EHS research through ARRA (described in Section 4 of this document), NIEHS will provide a $9 million increase to expand its NanoHealth and Safety Initiative. With these 2010 funds, NIEHS will support research to link more precisely the physical and chemical properties of nanomaterials with biological response, thus supplying critical data for hazard and risk assessment. To support the goals of this program, NIEHS is establishing collaborations with the NIH/National Cancer Institute's Nanotechnology Characterization Laboratory for physical characterization of nanomaterials and with the Cancer Biomedical Informatics Grid (CaBIG®) NanoLab for data storage.

NIOSH: NIOSH has focused resources on priorities across the NIOSH Nanotechnology Research Program. The 2011 Budget includes an increase in this program of more than 70 percent over 2010, enabling expansion of research to address major research gaps identified in the NIOSH Nanotechnology Progress Report (http://www.cdc.gov/niosh/docs/2010-104/) and in the *Strategic Plan for NIOSH Nanotechnology Research and Guidance* (http://www.cdc.gov/niosh/docs/2010-105/).

NIST: The President's 2011 Budget for NIST will continue to support research in nanotechnology, including a doubling of the budget for EHS aspects of nanotechnology (PCA 7, from $3.6 million in 2010 to $7.3 million in 2011, including a $4 million new initiative request) and significant new investments in support of the NNI Signature Initiatives focused on nanomanufacturing ($5 million new initiative request) and solar energy. NIST's expanded nanotechnology EHS program will provide the measurement science and technology (reference materials, documentary standards, reference data, instruments, and transferable methods and models) essential for science-based risk assessment and risk management of nanomaterials by regulatory agencies and industry. NIST will target its nanotechnology EHS program to measurements of dynamic physico-chemical and toxicological properties of key nanomaterials and release of these nanomaterials during manufacturing processes and from products throughout full product life cycles. NIST will coordinate and collaborate with other agencies and industry to establish linkages between physico-chemical properties and hazard and exposure effects in biological systems, the environment, and the workplace. NIST's nanomanufacturing research will focus on establishing measurements and methods to efficiently assemble products that integrate together billions or more of nanoscale devices with disparate functions over large areas. The energy-related program will target the nanoscale measurement science and tools needed to accelerate breakthroughs in third-generation photovoltaic solar cell technologies.

NSF: The 2011 NSF request includes an increase to $32.2 million to support new concepts for PCA 5, nanomanufacturing, such as high-rate synthesis and processing of nanostructures, nanostructured catalysts, nanobiotechnology methods, fabrication methods for devices, and assembly of devices into nanosystems and then into larger-scale structures of relevance in industry and in the medical field. R&D is aimed at enabling scaled-up, reliable, cost-effective manufacturing of nanoscale materials, structures, devices, and systems. A special focus will be creating active nanostructures and complex nanosystems (PCA 3).

The investment will emphasize (1) new tools for measuring and restructuring matter for production purposes; (2) hierarchical manufacturing of nanosystems by assembling nanoscale components into new architectures and fundamentally new products; (3) manufacturing by design using new computer principles, computer simulations, and nanoinformatics; and (4) hybrid nanomanufacturing, including nanobiotechnology and nanostructured catalysts. An overall goal will be advancing nanomanufacturing methods supporting sustainable development. NSF will strengthen its support for the National Nanomanufacturing Network composed of four Nanoscale Science and Engineering Centers in order to better support innovation and to partner and implement the research results with industry, medical institutions, and other government agencies.

In addition:

* NSF will continue to increase its investment in nanotechnology-related environmental, health, and safety research (PCA 7), by using core programs in relevant areas and a separate program solicitation.

- Partnerships with small businesses in the United States in the areas of nanomanufacturing and commercialization (PCA 5) will be strengthened while maintaining about the same level of NSF investment.

- The NSF 2011 request includes $140.1 million for PCA 1 (fundamental nanoscale phenomena and processes), a reduction of about $12 million compared to 2010. Some funds resulting from this reduction have transitioned into other PCAs as part of the competitive planning process in each NSF directorate.

- Several investments in major research facilities and instrumentation acquisition (PCA 6) will be reduced, since relevant investments made in previous years have taken effect and the research infrastructure is reasonably well established.

USDA/FS: Planned 2011 agency funding for nanotechnology research is focused on cellulosic nanomaterials derived from forest-based materials and remains at the $5.4 million level. The balance of USDA/FS investments by PCA remain unchanged from 2010, with investments in PCAs 1, 2, 3, 4, and 5 (fundamental nanoscale phenomena and processes; nanomaterials; nanoscale devices and systems; instrumentation research, metrology, and standards; and nanomanufacturing, respectively).

USDA/NIFA: The USDA National Institute of Food and Agriculture will continue its balanced investment by supporting research, development, education, and outreach activities in seven of the eight PCAs (see budget tables with PCA distributions). The primary emphases will remain in nanoscale devices and systems (PCA 3) for agricultural and food applications; nanomaterials and nanoscale biomaterials (PCA 2); fundamental nanoscale phenomena and processes (PCA 1); and environment, health, and safety (PCA 7). One new contribution, although small in total dollars, is an increase in PCA 4 for instrumentation research, metrology, and standards for nanotechnology. This is in recognition of the need to characterize engineered nanoscale materials under background environments in various agricultural and food applications.

Utilization of SBIR and STTR Programs to Advance Nanotechnology

As called for by the 21st Century Nanotechnology Research and Development Act, this report includes information on use of the Small Business Innovation Research (SBIR) and Small Business Technology Transfer (STTR) programs in support of nanotechnology development. Five NNI agencies—DOD, NSF, NIH, DOE, and NASA—have both SBIR and STTR programs. In addition to these agencies, EPA, NIOSH, NIST, and USDA have SBIR programs. Table 7 shows 2004 through 2008 (the latest year for which data is available) agency funding for SBIR and STTR awards for nanotechnology R&D. USDA/FS reported nanotechnology-related SBIR funding for the first time in 2008.

Some NNI agencies (e.g., EPA and NIH) have nanotechnology-specific topics in their SBIR and STTR solicitations. Some (e.g., NIH and NSF) have had topical or applications-oriented solicitations for which many awardees have proposed nanotechnology-based innovations. All told, with this revised data for 2004–2008, the NNI agencies have funded over $390 million in nanotechnology-related SBIR and STTR awards since 2004.

Table 7: 2004–2008 Agency SBIR and STTR Awards (dollars in millions)															
	2004			**2005**			**2006**			**2007**			**2008**		
	SBIR	**STTR**	**Total**	**SBIR**	**STTR**	**Total**	**SBIR**	**STTR**	**Total**	**SBIR**	**STTR**	**Total**	**SBIR**	**STTR**	**Total**
DOE	6.8	2.8	9.6	7.7	0.4	8.1	18.2	1.6	19.8	17.4	0.8	18.2	13.8	2.7	16.5
NSF	11.9	0.9	12.8	12.1	5.5	17.6	13.9	1.8	15.7	13.4	3.8	17.2	10.5	7.5	18.0
DHHS/NIH	9.3	2.6	11.9	11.1	5.2	16.3	15.1	2.1	17.2	18.4	1.1	19.5	29.3	1.8	31.1
DOD	10.5	6.9	17.4	7.5	5.5	13	12.6	5.6	18.2	8.4	4.2	12.6	19.8	2.3	22.1
DOC/NIST	0.5	0.0	0.5	0.1	0.0	0.1	0.1	0.0	0.1	0.3	0.0	0.3	0.4	0.0	0.4
EPA	0.6	0.0	0.6	1.0	0.0	1.0	1.2	0.0	1.2	0.5	0.0	0.5	0.7	0.0	0.7
DHHS/NIOSH	0.0	0.0	0.0	0.0	0.0	0.0	0.1	0.0	0.1	0.1	0.0	0.1	0.4	0.0	0.4
NASA	7.2	0.6	7.8	6.0	0.0	6.0	12.1	1.5	13.6	11.7	1.5	13.2	6.2	0.8	7.0
USDA/FS	0.0	0.0	0.0	0.0	0.0	0.0	0.0	0.0	0.0	0.0	0.0	0.0	0.3	0.0	0.3
USDA/NIFA	0.8	0.0	0.8	1.0	0.0	1.0	0.7	0.0	0.7	1.1	0.0	1.1	0.6	0.0	0.6
TOTAL	**47.6**	**13.8**	**61.4**	**46.5**	**16.6**	**63.1**	**74.0**	**12.6**	**86.6**	**71.3**	**11.4**	**82.7**	**81.9**	**15.1**	**97.0**

3. Agency Interests in Nanotechnology R&D

Introduction

In 1999 hearings held by the House Subcommittee on Basic Research of the Committee on Science to determine the nation's interest in nanotechnology, Chairman Nick Smith concluded that because "nanotechnology holds promise for breakthroughs in health, manufacturing, agriculture, energy use, and national security... it is sufficient information to aggressively address funding of this field." Shortly afterwards, the White House announced the National Nanotechnology Initiative, and in August 2000, the Subcommittee on Nanoscale Science, Engineering and Technology (NSET) was constituted as part of the NSTC Committee on Technology specifically to facilitate interagency collaboration on nanoscale R&D and to provide a framework for setting Federal R&D budget priorities. The NSET Subcommittee member agencies with budgets dedicated to nanotechnology R&D continue to fund these programs because the work done so far continues to support the early assumptions about the value of this growing scientific endeavor. The agencies describe below their individual interests in nanotechnology R&D, as they collectively contribute by various means to the welfare of the nation and to their respective agency missions and responsibilities.

Consumer Product Safety Commission (CPSC)

As more consumer products employ nanotechnology, concerns are increasing regarding the potential health effects associated with human exposure to this technology. There is a growing use of compounds or materials that have been produced using nanotechnologies that directly manipulate matter at the atomic level and fabrication of materials that could not have been produced in the past. Although these nanomaterials may have the same chemical composition as non-nanomaterials, at the nanoscale these nanomaterials may demonstrate different physical and chemical properties, and they may behave differently in the environment and the human body. Members of the U.S. Congress have stated that they recognize nanotechnology as a new technology utilized in the manufacture of consumer products, and that they expect the Commission to review the utilization and safety of its application in consumer products consistent with the Commission's mission. In support of that mission, CPSC has requested additional funding in 2011 to collect data on nanomaterials use in consumer products

Department of Defense (DOD)

DOD considers nanotechnology to have high and growing potential to contribute to the warfighting capabilities of the nation. Because of the broad and interdisciplinary nature of nanotechnology, DOD views it as an enabling technology area that should receive the highest level of corporate attention and coordination. These priorities are described in the most recent Department of Defense Research and Engineering Strategy, which can be accessed online at http://www.dod.mil/ddre/doc /Strategic_Plan_Final.pdf. DOD Basic Research acknowledges that realizing the potential of nanotechnology is a key research objective for the department. In particular, nanotechnology is an enabling technology for the new classes of sensors (such as novel focal plane arrays), communications, and information processing systems needed for qualitative improvements in persistent surveillance. The DOD also invests in nanotechnology for advanced energetic materials, photocatalytic coatings, active microelectronic devices, and a wide array of other promising technologies. The DOD nanotechnology program is based on coordinated planning and federated execution among the military departments and agencies (components) (e.g., the Defense Advanced Research Projects Agency and the Defense Threat

Reduction Agency). Nanotechnology currently represents a scientifically and technologically advanced research theme that has proven and expected value toward enhancing defense capabilities.

DOD does not establish funding targets for nanotechnology, which has proven to be effectively competitive based on its contributions to meeting needs and providing opportunities for future capability. New projects are awarded on a competitive basis, and as a result, the balance of investment can change from historical levels and predictions. Nonetheless, based on the state of nanoscience and nanotechnology research and development, the DOD expects that its primary emphasis will remain in fundamental nanoscale phenomena and processes (PCA 1), nanoscale devices and systems (PCA 3), and nanomaterials (PCA 2). Historically, DOD's Technology Base (Budget Activity 1–3) investment in nanotechnology has been approximately 50% Basic Research, about 40% Applied Research, and about 10% Advanced Technology Development. The bulk of the Small Business Innovation Research (SBIR)/Small Business Technology Transfer (STTR) investment in nanotechnology would be categorized as functionally similar to Applied Research, although with a strong, direct commercializable product or process aspect more analogous to Advanced Technology Development. The current expectation is that these overall percentages will be continued through 2011. As nanotechnology research areas and tools providers continue to mature, growth can be expected in Applied Research and Advanced Technology Development efforts. Maturation of specific products in commercial programs often occurs because of DOD-supported Basic and Applied Research efforts that have increased the knowledge and general technology base. For this reason, continued robust support is important for foundational research in an area that can be valuable to DOD and the nation.

DOD supports competitive research and development in nanotechnology to sustain and increase U.S. technological advantage and general capabilities in warfighting and peacekeeping operations. This provides a very broad front for nanotechnology efforts that are included in DOD programs. An excellent overview of DOD emphasis in nanotechnology may be gained by reviewing the agendas for the upcoming and historical Nanotechnology for Defense Conferences at the website https://www.usasymposium.com/nano/default.htm. The following foci of the 2009 conference provide a good example of the areas that DOD finds topical: (1) Nanomaterials and Technology for Energy Conversion and Storage, (2) Nanomaterials and Technology for Electronics and EM Sensing, (3) Nanomaterials and Technology for Structural Components, and (4) The Interface between Nano/Bio and its Potential Utility.

Department of Energy (DOE)

DOE views nanoscience and nanotechnology as having a vitally important role to play in solving the energy and climate change challenges faced by the nation. This broad and diverse field of research and development will likely have dramatic impact on future technologies for solar energy collection and conversion, energy storage, alternative fuels, and energy efficiency, to name just a few. DOE has participated in the NNI since its inception in 2001 and maintains a strong commitment to the initiative, which has served as an effective and valuable way of spotlighting needs and targeting resources in this critical emerging area. It continues to provide a crucial locus for interagency communication and collaboration, and an impetus for coordinated planning. Overall investment in physical sciences has been spurred by the NNI, and the research and infrastructure successes have clearly made the United States the world leader in this area, with many other nations seeking to emulate this initiative.

DOE funding spans all eight program component areas of the NNI, with the majority falling into three categories: fundamental phenomena and processes (PCA 1), nanomaterials (PCA 2), and major research facilities and instrumentation acquisition (PCA 6). In the latter category the DOE investment is significantly larger than that of any other agency, due primarily to the planning, construction, and operation of five Nanoscale Science Research Centers (NSRCs) located at DOE laboratories. The NSRCs operate as user facilities, with access based on submission of proposals that are reviewed by independent evaluation boards, and at no cost for non-proprietary work. The NSRCs support synthesis, processing, fabrication, and analysis at the nanoscale and are designed to be state-of-the-art user centers for interdisciplinary nanoscale research, serving as an integral part of DOE's comprehensive nanoscience program that encompasses new science, new tools, and new computing capabilities.

Department of Homeland Security (DHS)

DHS interests in nanoscience and associated areas are mostly materials-related, but the agency is making inroads into device applications as well this year. The applications for the efforts described below are in explosives detection for enhanced security for aviation, mass transit, and first responders:

- *Materials toolbox*: These efforts are focused on the development of materials systems that allow systematic control of chemical and structural features from molecular scales (functional groups) through nano- and microscales. The ability to precisely tune material properties is critical for successful development of improved active sensor surfaces and analyte collection substrates as well as development of novel sensing structures and arrays.

- *Advanced preconcentrators*: The DHS Science and Technology (S&T) Directorate is currently investigating the development of high-performance preconcentrators for use in next-generation detection systems. The focus of these efforts is the development of nano- and microscale materials that enable radio frequency (RF) and optical control of device temperature. To date, several functional prototypes have been demonstrated. Commercialization of these devices is currently being pursued.

- *Advanced sensing platforms*: Work on the development of multimodal carbon nanotube sensing platforms continues with industry partners. The emphasis of these efforts is on development of manufacturing techniques for low-cost sensor platforms.

Department of Justice/National Institute of Justice (DOJ/NIJ)

The NIJ investment in nanotechnology furthers the Department's mission through sponsoring research that provides objective, independent, evidence-based knowledge and tools to meet the challenges of crime and justice, particularly at the state and local levels. New projects are awarded on a competitive basis, and therefore, total investment may change each fiscal year. However, NIJ continues to view nanotechnology as an integral component of its research and development portfolio.

Director of National Intelligence (DNI)

The National Reconnaissance Office (NRO) R&D program focus emphasizes developments in electronics, structural materials, and power generation and energy storage devices:

- In electronics, the program is emphasizing large-scale carbon nanotube (CNT)-based memory, CNT-based logic devices, and CNT field-effect transistors. CNT-based electronics foundry materials and processes are completely compatible with operations in a standard silicon foundry. Additionally, CNT electronics are inherently radiation-hardened, nonvolatile in nature, and extremely low in power consumption because states are retained by van der Waals forces. The 2011 program will emphasize increased density for memory devices, progressing from the current 4 million bit memory to 64 million bit and 512 million bit memories for space-based operations. Such progress represents a 100-fold improvement of current space-survivable memories.

- For structural components, the program will emphasize the use of carbon nanotube threads and yarns to produce conductive wires, impact- and bullet-proof panels, support struts, electromagnetic suppression boxes, and thermal conductive and thermal-electrical converters. Conductive wire research proposes to exceed the conductivity of copper wires while removing up to 80% of the weight of a signal or power harness. Research to produce CNT panels to withstand high-velocity space debris and to stop large-caliber bullets will be conducted. Research to use functionalized CNT yarns to transport heat away from electronic components and convert the heat to power for space systems will target a 12% energy conversion efficiency.

- Nanotechnology R&D for power generation and energy storage devices emphasizes topics such as quartz nanorods as an improved solar cell cover glass, indium arsenide quantum dot technology for higher-efficiency solar cells, and carbon nanotube electrodes and additives to improve the performance and safety of lithium-ion (Li-ion) batteries. The goal for power generation is to increase solar cell efficiency from the present 33% to 47% for monolithic cells in a space environment. Power storage R&D aims to replace 9 nickel-hydride batteries with a single Li-ion battery capable of 10 years of orbital life.

Environmental Protection Agency (EPA)

The 2011 President's budget request will further EPA's generation of decision-support information to promote the safe development, use, and disposal/recycling of products that contain manufactured nanoscale materials. Sustainability is a theme that runs through the EPA nanotechnology research program. Using green chemistry and life-cycle assessment approaches, EPA is investigating how nanomaterials behave in the environment, how nanomaterial properties may be modified or exposure controls implemented to minimize and manage potential risks from products containing nanomaterials, as well as ways to minimize inputs, including energy usage, during the production of nanomaterials.

EPA's Nanomaterial Research Strategy (http://www.epa.gov/nanoscience) guides EPA's nanomaterial research. The strategy builds on and is consistent with the scientific needs identified in the 2006 NEHI Working Group report *Environmental, Health, and Safety Research Needs for Engineered Nanoscale Materials* (http://www.nano.gov/NNI_EHS_research_needs.pdf) and on the 2007 EPA Nanotechnology White Paper (http://www.epa.gov/osa/nanotech.htm). EPA's research activities are coordinated across the U.S. Federal Government through the NNI and internationally within the Organisation for Economic Cooperation and Development (OECD).

Since 2001, EPA has played a leading role in supporting research and setting research directions to develop environmental applications for nanotechnology as well as to understand the potential human health and environmental implications of nanotechnology. The EPA has provided such leadership through its Science to Achieve Results (STAR) grant program and through contracts to small businesses under its Small Business Innovation Research program, both of which have developed a cadre of highly skilled researchers and engineers with expertise in the area of environmental nanotechnology. EPA's own research laboratories are conducting targeted research to inform decisions related to nanotechnology and the environment. EPA collaborates in research with other Federal agencies, as well as internationally by issuing joint grant solicitations with other governments (such as the United Kingdom and the European Commission) and by EPA's own researchers joining other nations in the international testing program being conducted under the auspices of OECD. As the use of nanomaterials increases, EPA will continue to determine how to best leverage advances in nanotechnology to enhance public health and environmental protection, as well as to improve scientific knowledge to understand and avoid any possible negative impacts of nanomaterials on the environment. The goal is to foster technological advances that maximize benefits to society by minimizing environmental impacts.

Food and Drug Administration (FDA)

Nanomaterials often have chemical, physical, or biological properties that are different from those of their larger-scale counterparts. Such differences may include altered magnetic, electrical, or optical properties, structural integrity, and chemical or biological activity. Because of researchers' ability to engineer such properties, nanoscale materials have great potential for use in a vast array of products, including FDA-regulated products intended to protect and promote public health. Also, because of some of their special properties, nanomaterials may pose different issues for toxicologic, safety, and effectiveness assessments. As such, there is a growing need for scientific information and tools to help better predict or detect potential impacts of such changes on human health.

FDA nanotechnology investments in prior and future years are focused on enabling the agency to characterize nanotechnology-based products; develop models for safety and efficacy assessment; and study the behavior of nanomaterials in biological systems and their effects on human health. These investments will support responsible development of nanotechnology.

FDA also continues to foster and develop collaborative relationships with other Federal agencies through the NNI, as well as with sister regulatory agencies, international organizations, healthcare professionals, industry, consumers, and other stakeholders. These collaborations allow information to be exchanged efficiently and serve to identify research needed to address the use nanomaterials in FDA-regulated products. Although FDA activities will likely be relevant to all four NNI goals, FDA efforts are primarily focused on the goal to facilitate responsible development of nanotechnology in three FDA priority areas of (1) building laboratory and product testing capacity, (2) establishing scientific staff development and training, and (3) engaging in collaborative and interdisciplinary research to address product characterization and safety.

National Institutes of Health (NIH)

Nanotechnology is capable of producing tools that can help NIH advance opportunities to develop novel diagnostics and therapeutics as well as tools enabling research at cellular and sub-cellular levels.

The emergence of nanotechnology has opened a new era of design-driven research into the development of unique 3D nanomaterials and nanostructures with the potential for significant clinical impact across a range of diseases and disorders. The NIH continues to expand its support for nanoscale engineering of multifunctional systems for drug and gene therapy, nanostructures for tissue engineering, and a variety of other biomedical applications, in addition to research tools that aid in understanding the underlying causes of diseases. Progress continues in development of sensors that are both selective and highly sensitive, for early diagnosis of disease (when disease is easiest to treat). Some of these sensors involve imaging techniques that pinpoint chemical and biochemical processes that are characteristic of specific diseases; these exams complement current anatomical imaging to provide essential information for early diagnosis. Others may be used as lab tests that identify early markers of diseases such as cancer or heart disease from a small drop of blood or saliva. Multifunctional nanoparticles are being developed to deliver conventional or novel therapeutics directly to the specific tissues or cells in the body that are affected by disease, sparing healthy cells from drug side-effects. Some of these particles may help doctors to detect how much medicine is needed at a particular time, and to dispense only that dose at the time and location in the body where it is needed.

Nanotechnology-based research tools are being used to better understand the causes and course of diseases, and the effects of genetics and environment on individual patients. NIH plays a substantial role in developing understanding of how to design nanoparticles so they can be safe to use both for manufacturing and for medical treatments. NIH research projects are awarded through rigorous peer review by a variety of mechanisms that range from large, multidisciplinary centers as components of agency-designed programs, to projects submitted by individual investigators who compete for funding of their most creative and promising ideas.

Commercialization is facilitated through funding of SBIR/STTR grants and programs at the various NIH institutes that encourage universities and companies to collaborate, and by providing resources and expertise to test novel formulations for safety and biological activity. Ongoing clinical testing of numerous potential products is an encouraging sign that the investment is paying off and continues to be highly productive.

National Institute for Occupational Safety and Health (NIOSH)

Since the inception of the NIOSH nanotechnology program in 2004, NIOSH researchers have conducted pioneering studies on the hazards of manufactured nanomaterials, real-world exposures to workers, and the effectiveness of exposure mitigation techniques such as respiratory protection. The NIOSH Nanotechnology Field Research project (http://www.cdc.gov/niosh/topics/nanotech/field.html), a partnership effort with industry, has been a highly successful and popular resource for hosting organizations and for NIOSH. These studies provide detailed information facilitating risk assessment and management and continue to remind all involved that prudent measures should be taken in mitigating potential exposures to nanomaterials in the workplace.

NIOSH focuses its activities on evaluating the potential hazards of select nanomaterials, assessing human exposures in workplace and potential health risk, evaluating controls and risk management practices for safe handling of nanomaterials, and developing guidance on medical screening and evaluation of workers. Any increase in funding would support research to address the following areas:

- NIOSH toxicology studies have provided better understanding of the ways in which some types of nanoparticles may enter the body and interact with the body's organ systems; the breadth and depth of such research efforts have been limited to a few nanoparticle types. More types of nanoparticles need to be assessed for characteristics and properties relevant for predicting potential health risks.

- NIOSH field investigators have assessed exposure to engineered nanoparticles in some workplaces, but little data exist on the extent and magnitude of exposures to other types of nanoparticles in workplaces that manufacture or use nanomaterials, nanostructures, and nanodevices.

- NIOSH guidance is a first step toward controlling nanoparticles in the workplace; however, more research is needed on the efficacy and specificity of engineering and work-practice control measures. Significantly more field research is needed to develop guidance based on evaluating possible short- and long-term health risks in nanotechnology workers, and to develop guidance for medical studies and for prospective medical epidemiologic studies.

- The utility of nanotechnology to support development of new technologies (such as sensors, more efficient filters, and better protective materials) that can enhance the protection of workers requires further research and development.

Internationally, NIOSH will expand its support and leadership activities in nanotechnology safety and health in the World Health Organization (WHO), the United Nations Institute for Training and Research (UNITAR), the Organisation for Economic Cooperation and Development (OECD), and the

International Organization for Standardization (ISO). In addition, NIOSH is providing support to the International Council on Nanotechnology (ICON) project "Good Nano Guide" (http://goodnanoguide.org/).

National Institute of Standards and Technology (NIST)

Advancing nanoscale measurement science, standards, and nanotechnology is an important component of NIST's mission to promote U.S. innovation and industrial competitiveness. From leading cutting-edge research to coordinating the development of standards that promote trade, NIST's programs in nanotechnology directly impact priorities important to the nation's economy and well-being. The nanotechnology-related research conducted in NIST's laboratories develops measurements, standards, and data crucial to a wide range of industries and Federal agencies, from the development of advanced spectroscopic methods needed to increase efficiency in advanced photovoltaics, to the development of the standard reference materials and data necessary to accurately quantify and measure the presence and impact of nanomaterials in the environment. NIST further supports the U.S. nanotechnology enterprise from discovery to production through its Center for Nanoscale Science and Technology (CNST), established in 2007. The CNST creates the next generation of nanoscale measurement instruments, makes them available through collaboration, and provides rapid access to a world-class, shared-use nanofabrication facility, the NanoFab. NIST's Technology Innovation Program is investing in the development of transformational technologies necessary to advance the large-scale manufacture of nanomaterials. In coordination with the private sector, NIST provides the technical foundation and leadership to the development of international nanotechnology standards—standards that are a key to opening new markets and facilitating trade and commerce.

National Science Foundation (NSF)

The National Science Foundation supports nanoscale science and engineering in all disciplines throughout all its research and education directorates as a means to promote discovery and innovation and integrate various fields of research. NNI funding provides a source of increased interdisciplinarity for about 5,000 active awards that represent more than 10% of the overall NSF portfolio. About 10,000 students and teachers are educated and trained in nanoscale science and engineering each year. Over 100 small businesses were funded to perform research and product development in nanotechnology through the SBIR/STTR programs.

The National Science Foundation supports upstream research and education in all areas of nanoscale science and engineering, leading to a flexible infrastructure and educational pipeline at the national level. It also advances nanotechnology innovation through a variety of translational research programs and by partnering with industry, states, and other agencies. The investment of $418 million in 2010 will support over 4,000 active projects, over 30 large centers grouped in ten networks, and 10,000 students and teachers. About $20 million has been allocated in 2009 for nanotechnology-related SBIR/STTR projects based on merit review; this opportunity will continue in 2011.

Fundamental changes envisioned through nanotechnology have required a long-term R&D vision. NSF sponsored the first initiative dedicated to nanoparticles in 1991, the 1997–1999 program Partnership in Nanotechnology, and it produced the 1999 interagency report *Nanotechnology Research Directions: Vision for Nanotechnology in the Next Decade* that was adopted as an official NSTC document in 2000.

NSF's nanotechnology research is supported primarily through grants to individuals, teams, and centers at U.S. academic institutions. The efforts in team and center projects have been particularly fruitful because nanoscale research and education are inherently interdisciplinary pursuits, often combining elements of chemistry, biology, manufacturing, physics, optics, and photonics, and nearly every other field of basic science. An illustration is the Nanotechnology Computational Network that has reached 100,000 research and education users annually.

A main NSF funding increase in 2011 is for nanomanufacturing to support new concepts for high-rate synthesis and processing of nanostructures, nanostructured catalysts, nanobiotechnology methods, and methods for fabricating devices, assembling them into nanosystems, and then into larger-scale structures of relevance in industry and in the medical field. R&D is aimed at enabling scaled-up, reliable, cost-effective manufacturing of nanoscale materials, structures, devices, and systems. The National Nanomanufacturing Network is organized around four centers collaborating with other NNI agencies. Environmental, health, and safety implications of nanotechnology, including development of predictive toxicity of nanomaterials, will be investigated in three dedicated multidisciplinary centers and in over 60 other smaller groups.

U.S. Department of Agriculture, Forest Service (USDA/FS)

Forests are a major strategic asset of the United States and provide critically important economic and environmental benefits, including jobs in rural America, recreation, watershed management, wildlife habitat, and other critically important ecosystem services. Trees, the basis for the U.S. forest products sector, are a sustainable, renewable resource that helps mitigate climate change through the sequestration of carbon—both in the growth of forest biomass and in forest products—and they represent a vast storehouse of renewable feedstock for production of biomass-derived fuels, power, and chemicals. Each year over 200 million tons of wood are converted to over $250 billion of products, employing over 1.4 million Americans and representing about 6 percent of America's manufacturing Gross Domestic Product. Despite the large tonnages used, the United States harvests less than one percent of its total standing forest biomass each year, and the volume of annual growth over harvest ratio in America's forests is over 2:1.

Nanotechnology has enormous promise to bring about fundamental changes and significant benefit to the nation. Nanotechnology offers the way to efficiently and effectively capitalize on a major strategic national asset to make forest-derived materials the "materials of choice for the 21st century." Wood from trees is made up of nanodimensional building blocks that: (1) have strength properties greater than Kevlar® and piezoelectric properties equivalent to quartz, (2) can be manipulated to produce photonic structures, (3) are remarkably uniform in size and shape, (4) possess self-assembly properties, and (5) can be renewably produced in quantities of tens of millions of tons. Recognizing the importance of this emerging opportunity, U.S. Department of Agriculture Forest Service R&D (FS R&D) has taken steps to establish a foundation in forest products nanotechnology research and development. Through participation in the NNI and representation on the NSET Subcommittee, FS R&D is partnering with other Federal entities (e.g., NIST, NSF, DOE, DOD), industry, and academia to develop the precompetitive science and technology critical to the economic and sustainable production and use of new high-value, nanotechnology-enabled, forest-based materials and products.

The U.S. forest products industry, through the American Forest & Paper Association Agenda 2020 Technology Alliance, has signed a memorandum of understanding with the NSET Subcommittee to form a Cooperative Board for Advancing Nanotechnology (CBAN). The U.S. forest products industry is in a unique position to tap the huge potential nanotechnology provides, in two primary ways. First, by becoming a user of nanotechnology materials and components in its products and processes, the industry can upgrade its processes and produce new high-performance consumer products from lignocellulosic-based materials in a safe and sustainable manner. Second, the industry intends to become a producer and developer of novel, sustainable nanomaterials to replace nonsustainable materials such as those from fossil fuels. For example, use of wood-derived nano-dimensional cellulose in nanocomposites will allow the production of much lighter-weight, hyper-strength, multifunctional materials to replace metals and plastics, with widespread application in many industry sectors. Other potential applications include electronic displays and microelectronic devices; clear armor; self-sterilizing and self-healing surfaces; pharmaceutical products; and intelligent wood- and paper-based products with an array of microsensors and nanosensors built in to measure forces, loads, moisture levels, temperature, pressure, chemical emissions, and attack by mold and wood-decaying fungi.

Recognizing that the values of wood and wood-based materials at the nanoscale are virtually untapped, industry technology leaders working with government and academia have developed a vision for nanotechnology and identified three priority focus areas:

- Creating new revenue streams from production of new generations of high-value, high-performance, innovative nanotechnology-enabled products and forest-derived nanomaterials

- Improving the strength/weight performance of traditional paper- and wood-based structural materials

- Developing new value-added, multifunctional features for paper and forest products

FS R&D is continuing to focus on developing its internal wood-based nanotechnology research capacities and to effectively partner with industry, academia, and other Federal entities. The National Nanotechnology Initiative is critical to advancing this public-private-university partnership. In addition, the NNI effectively addresses nanotechnology-focused environmental, health, and safety issues as well as ethical, legal, and societal issues—areas where FS R&D has little or no expertise or capacity to carry out credible work.

U.S. Department of Agriculture, National Institute of Food and Agriculture (USDA/NIFA)

The National Institute of Food and Agriculture (NIFA) of the U.S. Department of Agriculture (USDA) was established by the 2008 Farm Bill to serve the nation's needs by supporting exemplary research, education, and extension that addresses challenges facing the nation. Research enables Americans to develop the knowledge needed to innovatively solve many critical societal issues. Education strengthens schools and universities to train the next generation of scientists, educators, producers, and citizens. Extension brings the knowledge gained and technology development through research and education to the people who need it most—in the United States and around the world.

NIFA's current priority areas include (1) global food security and hunger, (2) climate change, (3) sustainable energy, (4) childhood obesity, and (5) food safety. Nanoscale science and nanotechnology has demonstrated relevance and great potential to enable revolutions in broad agriculture and food systems, including plant production and products; animal health, production, and products; food safety, nutrition, health, and wellness; renewable energy, natural resources, and environment; agriculture systems and technology; and agriculture economics and rural communities. The agency's nanotechnology research has broadly contributed to the NNI PCAs, with primary emphasis on fundamental nanoscale phenomena and processes (PCA 1), nanomaterials (PCA 2), nanoscale devices and systems (PCA 3), and environment, health, and safety (PCA 7).

In particular, NIFA's nanoscale science and nanotechnology research has focused its investment on detection and intervention technologies for enhancing food safety and agricultural biosecurity; effective and safe delivery of bioactives in functional foods for improving human health and wellness; and product traceability, identity preservation, and tracking to embrace the continuous advancement of information technology for better decision making through the Agriculture and Food Research Initiative (AFRI), NIFA's flagship competitive grants program. AFRI also has supported research to assess and analyze the perceptions and acceptance of nanotechnology applications in food and agriculture and nanotechnology-based products by the general public, the agriculture producers, the processing industry, and other stakeholders, using appropriate social science tools. Future opportunities for research investment include using plants or animals (or cells or cultures of plants and animals) to produce specifically constructed nanomaterials at low cost in genetically engineered organisms. NIFA's SBIR program also supports innovative nanotechnology research and development throughout its broad topic areas.

4. Progress Towards Achieving NNI Goals and Priorities

NNI Contributions to Administration Goals for the Nation

The NSET Subcommittee's coordination of member agencies' NNI programs is guided by and contributes to many of the Administration's goals for the nation in terms of the economy, energy, the environment, technology, and national defense, among other areas. Details of NNI contributions in these areas are provided in the *NNI Supplement to the President's 2010 Budget*; please see http://www.nano.gov/NNI_2010_budget_supplement.pdf, pages 13–14.

Activities Relating to the Four NNI Goals

As called for in the 21st Century Nanotechnology Research and Development Act, the 2007 NNI Strategic Plan states that the interagency analysis of progress under the NNI will be provided in the annual NNI Supplement to the President's Budget. As indicated in the plan, the NNI's activities for 2009 and 2010 and plans for 2011 are reported here in terms of how they promote progress toward the four NNI goals. Goal-related activities are in turn reported in terms of two categories of activities: (1) individual agency activities and (2) coordinated activities, including engagement with other agencies and groups and activities external to the NNI, and international activities. A brief report of progress toward the NNI goals in terms of these two categories follows. *The activities described below are only selected highlights of current and planned work of the NNI member agencies and are not an all-inclusive description of ongoing NNI activities.*

Goal 1: Advance a world-class nanotechnology research and development program

The NNI member agencies have sustained a strategic investment in nanotechnology R&D, something that is widely recognized as essential for the development and successful exploitation of any emerging technology. The expanded investment by this Administration in nanotechnology will build on the foundation established over the past ten years and set the stage for transitioning the basic research discoveries into technologies and products for the benefit of our society and the nation's economy.

As indicated in the NNI Strategic Plan, the NNI is (1) sustaining a variety of complementary R&D investment pathways, including single-investigator research, multi-investigator and team efforts, interdisciplinary centers of excellence, and user facilities and networks; (2) mapping the leading edge of R&D by sponsoring topical and strategy-setting workshops; (3) coordinating the NNI research and development investments across multiple agencies; and (4) stimulating collaborations and interactions across agencies, disciplines, industrial sectors, and nations. Examples of efforts toward all four components of this goal are presented below.

Individual Agency Contributions to Goal 1

DOD: Specific examples of DOD investments in Goal 1 are as follows:

* Research in graphene focuses on the study, manipulation, and simulation of charge transport; the engineered synthesis of desired electronic properties; and device fabrication technology that will lead to understanding of the fundamental graphene device physics and technology for advancement of multifunctional electronic devices and establish an enabling science and technology in graphene nanoelectronics for commercial, public, and DOD benefits. The Army Research Laboratory hosted a 2-day workshop on graphene electronics in 2009 as the first in a series of workshops on this topic. The

workshop attracted 47 eminent scientists and researchers from academia and several DOD agencies as well as researchers from 5 leading industrial organizations.

- Research is conducted exploiting the ability to integrate unique properties of nanomaterials with conventional, industry-standard microfabrication and nanofabrication technology for the realization of novel actuators for microrobotics, small- and large-scale high-density energy storage and generation systems, and novel micro-initiator concepts for fuse applications. In 2010 this effort is expanded beyond nanoporous silicon to pursue the integration of currently incompatible microelectromechanical systems (MEMS) and nanoenergetic materials and processes, such as ink jet and thin film deposition techniques for an explosive chemical (RDX) and energetic intermetallic compositions.

- Organic nanomaterials for flexible and printed electronics and displays are being pursued by an Army team that has designed and synthesized nanoscale organic molecular pair structures that interact to form a charge separation across the pair, or a charge-transfer complex, that enhances charge transport.

- The area of bandgap engineering involves nanostructures such as quantum wells, superlattices, quantum dots, and nanopillars for a wide variety of applications including infrared imaging, energy generation and harvesting, and laser and light-emitting diode (LED) sources. The first quantum dot solar cells operating in the near-infrared (0.9 micron to 1.1 micron) wavelength range have been demonstrated this past year at the Army Research Laboratory. Material is being provided to the State University of New York at Stony Brook for minority carrier lifetime measurements in type II SLS (strained superlattice) structures for infrared detection.

- At the Army Communications-Electronics Research, Development, and Engineering Center (CERDEC) under the Breakthrough Antenna Technology program, research is being conducted to mature and develop printed conformal antennas utilizing artificial magnetic metamaterials. As part of this objective, a nanomaterials effort will synthesize up to eight different series of magnetic metal nanoparticles with dielectric shell coatings in kilogram-scale quantities. Included in this effort will be a characterization of each compound with respect to particle distribution and phase uniformity.

- The first significant improvement in thermoelectric power factors and overall thermoelectric performance was demonstrated by Office of Naval Research researchers in a nanocomposite of semi-metallic nanoparticles in a compound semiconductor matrix. The composite exhibited resonant states in the electronic band structure. This material's performance has been independently validated and has attracted industrial interest for automobile waste heat recovery.

DOE: The Department of Energy's support for the National Nanotechnology Initiative continues to come primarily from the DOE's Office of Science through support of fundamental R&D, instrumentation, and construction and operation of major research facilities. In 2010 the 46 new Energy Frontier Research Centers (EFRCs) that DOE awarded and initiated in 2009 are fully operational. These collaborative, multi-investigator, multi-institution research projects bring together interdisciplinary teams from universities, national labs, and industry to focus on energy-relevant fundamental science. A significant fraction of the EFRC research is classified as nanoscience, and that portion is reported in the budget figures provided.

In 2010, DOE will initiate an Energy Innovation Hub focused on solar fuels to continue to encourage collaboration and team science and to connect the research labs to the industrial world. An Energy Innovation Hub focused on batteries and energy storage is requested in 2011. It is expected that some portion of the research activities in both hubs will involve nanotechnology, and that portion has been estimated in the budget figures provided.

NIH (ARRA-Related Activities): NIH has received new funds for 2009 and 2010 as part of the American Recovery & Reinvestment Act (ARRA) of 2009. The ARRA Funds were distributed using various strategies and mechanisms to develop and implement critical research innovations to advance the research enterprise, stimulate future growth and investments, and advance public health and healthcare delivery. NIH initiatives were created to support this endeavor and have resulted in funding of nanotechnology R&D projects. These include the Challenge Grants (RC1), Grand Opportunity (GO) Grants, and Small Business Investments (RC3). A complete list of Funding Opportunity Announcements (FOAs) related to the ARRA is available at http://grants.nih.gov/recovery/. For a current listing of ARRA-funded nanotechnology projects, visit the NIH's Research Portfolio Online Reporting Tool (RePORT), accessible via http://report.nih.gov/recovery/ and conduct a keyword search on nanotechnology and ARRA for 2009 within the RePORTer box located at the left column.

Under the Recovery Act, NIH established a new program entitled "Research and Research Infrastructure Grand Opportunities" called the "GO" grants program (RFA-09-004). The purpose of the GO grants program is to support high-impact ideas that lend themselves to short-term funding and may lay the foundation for new fields of investigation. The GO grants program supports large-scale research projects that accelerate critical breakthroughs, early and applied research on cutting-edge technologies, and new approaches to improve the synergy and interactions among multidisciplinary and interdisciplinary research teams. Using this mechanism, for example, the NIH National Institute of General Medical Sciences (NIGMS) made 2-year awards to develop and refine methods for building multifunctional particles and probes that target and deliver chemical agents to locate, activate, image, or medicate targets within a cell or organism. A similar strategy was employed by the National Institute of Biomedical Imaging and Bioengineering (NIBIB), the National Cancer Institute (NCI), and the National Heart, Lung, and Blood Institute (NHLBI) to develop multifunctional delivery systems that combine imaging and therapeutic agents to diagnose and treat diseases (termed "theranostics") through the NIH Challenge Grants in Health and Science Research (RC1) solicitation (RFA-OD-09-003). The purpose of this new program was to fund projects that propose novel research in areas that address specific knowledge gaps, scientific opportunities, new technologies, data generation, or research methods in scientific areas identified by the institutes and centers of NIH through 2010. The NIH National Institute of Dental and Craniofacial Research (NIDCR) also utilized this RC1 mechanism to support R&D in developing new materials such as nanocomposites and smart self-healing materials to enhance restorative properties for dental needs (e.g., adhesives, improved durability, better aesthetics, and maximum biocompatibility) and such as nanostructured surfaces to control endogenous cells and processes *in vivo*. These awards complement NIDCR's recently issued 2009 RFA (Request for Applications) on "Harnessing Inflammation for Reconstruction of Oral and Craniofacial Tissues." Six awards were made at the end of 2009, totaling $3.45 million, to develop advanced bioengineering methodologies and/or nanotechnology-based tools and strategies for resolving acute and chronic inflammation and regenerating such tissues.

NIH/NIEHS increased its investment in understanding the potential health, safety, and environmental effects of engineered nanomaterials by awarding approximately $13 million over a two-year period through ARRA. NIEHS awarded 13 new two-year grants to develop better methods to assess exposure and health effects associated with nanomaterials. Ten of the grants were awarded through the NIH Grand Opportunities program announced in March 2009; see http://www.niehs.nih.gov/recovery/nanomaterial-go.cfm for details. Three were funded from the NIH Challenge Grants program. All 13 are aimed at developing reliable tools and approaches to determine the impact of engineered nanomaterials on biological systems and health outcomes.

NIH/NCI dedicated $7–8 million of its ARRA funding to pursuing further discovery and clinical translation in cancer nanotechnology. This funding supplemented operation of its Centers of Cancer Nanotechnology Excellence and Nanotechnology Platforms as well as covered selected Challenge (RC1) and Grand Opportunities (RC2) grants.

NIH's National Human Genome Research Institute (NHGRI) selected $1,000 Genome Sequencing Technology Development as its ARRA Signature Project. Nanotechnology is central to several awards made under this and other NHGRI ARRA funding. Included is a study on ethical challenges related to nanotechnology research.

NIH (Non-ARRA Activities): In 2010, NIBIB and NIEHS plan to co-fund a contract proposal in response to a recent solicitation to develop and launch a Federally curated interoperative registry designed to link existing databases that define physical, chemical, and other properties of nanomaterials for the community.

NIBIB also issued a 3-year program announcement in November 2008 entitled "Innovation in Molecular Imaging Probes" (PAR-09-016) that resulted in grants that will engineer nanoprobes or develop nanotechnology-enabled tools to detect and image specific molecular activities *in vivo* for clinical applications. This FOA is a follow-up of a previous NIH Common Fund RFA (RM-04-021 "Innovation in Molecular Imaging Probes").

In 2009, the NIBIB and NHLBI issued a 3-year FOA to support the development of novel, multifunctional delivery systems that can target the delivery of therapeutic agents to specific cells or compartments within cells, *in vivo*, and that possess imaging or sensing capabilities to track delivery and determine therapeutic efficacy. In addition to the real-time assessment of targeted therapy with enhanced efficacy, the identification of quantitative *in vivo* relationships between the carrier and cellular events must be determined, which in turn will lead to new engineering design principles at the nanoscale.

NIST: NIST's research program in nanotechnology is addressing national needs in energy, the environment, healthcare, information technology security, manufacturing, and physical infrastructure, as illustrated by the following examples:

- NIST is broadly applying quantum phenomenon at the nanoscale, including single-photon counting, single and entangled photon sources, and quantum coherence, to develop revolutionary devices for communications, sensing, and spectroscopy.

- Next-generation standards are being developed using nanotechnology, including new electrical resistance standards that exploit the unique quantum properties of graphene, and the first SI-traceable nanoindentation instrument for measuring mechanical properties at the nanoscale.

- NIST has developed a low-cost technique for measuring infrared light that is over 1,000 times more sensitive than existing instruments and is capable of measuring the infrared spectrum at single-photon levels emitted by fragile biomaterials and nanomaterials.

- NIST is developing next-generation chemical measurements with molecular- and atomic-scale resolution and will enhance its capabilities in 2010 with atom-probe tomography.

- NIST's ultralow-temperature (10 mK), ultrahigh-vacuum, high-magnetic-field (15 T), scanning probe microscope laboratory began operation in November 2009, capable of measuring quantum nanoelectronics phenomena with unprecedented spatial and energy resolution.

In 2010 the NIST Technology Innovation Program awarded $22.8 million in grants, primarily to small companies, to advance nanomanufacturing and create nanoscale devices and systems. NIST also awarded multiple ARRA grants supporting over $3 million of university nanotechnology research.

NSF: New efforts planned by NSF in 2011 for Goal 1 include the following:

- Planning and enhancing funding for the programs
  - Nanoelectronics for 2020 and Beyond
  - Nanotechnology for Regenerating the Human Body
  - Nanotechnology for Solar Energy Collection and Conversion
  - Nanostructured Catalysts for Green Manufacturing
  - Nanomanufacturing for Sustainable Development
- Enhancing funding for quantum information systems

USDA/NIFA: NIFA's Agriculture and Food Research Initiative nanotechnology research and development supports the agency's mission and its strategic goals. Currently, AFRI plans to support interdisciplinary, multifunctional projects in five grand societal challenge areas to achieve significant and measurable outcomes. The five goals are: (1) keep American agriculture competitive while ending world hunger, (2) improve nutrition and end child obesity, (3) improve food safety for all Americans, (4) secure America's energy future through renewable biofuels, and (5) mitigate and adapt agriculture to variations in climate. Nanoscale science, engineering, and nanotechnology will provide enabling tools to aid development of innovative solutions to these challenges.

USGS: USGS research in nanotechnology focuses in two areas. Work is underway to examine the fate and effects of nanotubes in sediment-dwelling organisms. Additionally, USGS scientists are examining the fate of nanoparticles in the aquatic environment. Some of this research concerns bacterially mediated production of quantum dots, and the remainder centers on the detection and fate of anthropogenically derived nanoparticles.

Coordinated Activities with Other Agencies and Other Institutions Contributing to Goal 1

DOD and the Edgewood Chemical Biological Center (ECBC): The Army Aviation and Missile Research Development and Engineering Center (AMRDEC) plans to coordinate with ECBC to test and validate AMRDEC-developed chemical/gas nanosensors.

NIH and the Chinese Academy of Sciences: The National Cancer Institute (NIH/NCI), the National Institute of Environmental Health Sciences (NIH/NIEHS), and the Chinese Academy of Sciences organized the "First Joint U.S.-China Symposium on Nanobiology and Nanomedicine" in Beijing, October 20–22, 2008; the follow-up meeting is to be held in Washington, DC, in 2010. The goal of the symposium was to exchange research experiences and consider possible collaborations in the areas of cancer nanotechnology (prevention, detection, and treatment of the disease), and the effects of exposure to nanomaterials on the general public and the environment. In the United States, over $1.5 billion/year of Federal support is dedicated to nanotechnology research and development (http://www.nano.gov /NNI_2010_budget_supplement.pdf). The Chinese government has established several nanotechnology research centers, including the National Center for Nanoscience and Technology in Beijing. In response to this rapidly maturing nanotechnology research base in China, this meeting and follow-up conversations concerning possible venues of interactions should produce joint projects leveraging strengths of efforts in both countries and promote exchanges of researchers.

NIH and U.S. and Indian cancer researchers: NCI participated in the 1st Indo-U.S. Cancer Nanotechnology Symposium in New Delhi, February 4–6, 2009. The meeting brought together researchers from India and the United States to discuss possible collaborations, student exchanges, and joint funding opportunities.

NIST, other agencies, industry, and universities: NIST co-sponsors workshops with a wide range of partners to identify measurement needs for nanotechnology. In 2009, workshops were held on Enabling Standards for Nanomaterial Characterization; Frontiers of Characterization and Metrology for Nanoelectronics; Calibrations and Standards for Nanomechanical Measurements; and Nanoscale Measurement Challenges for Energy Applications. In 2010, workshops are planned on Nano-Optics, Plasmonics, and Advanced Materials; and Metrology and Standards for Nanoelectronics.

NRO with DOD (Air Force) and NASA: The National Reconnaissance Office, the United States Air Force Space and Missile Center, and the Air Force Research Laboratory at Wright Patterson Air Force Base are coordinating and conducting joint electronic component R&D. NASA provides early demonstration flights for developed carbon nanotube electronics and radiation testing to qualify electronics for space operations.

NRO with DOD: The Office of the Secretary of Defense, Defense Production Act, monitors R&D success and aids to move pilot-scale plants to full production facilities for carbon nanotube materials for structural components.

NRO with DOE: Power generation and energy storage R&D is conducted with the Department of Energy National Renewable Energy Laboratory.

USDA/FS and industry: The USDA Forest Service has forged a strong working relationship with the U.S. Forest Products Industry, primarily through the American Forest & Paper Association (AF&PA) Agenda 2020 Technology Alliance. AF&PA includes most of the leading forest products companies in the United States. A common research, development, and deployment agenda has been identified with appropriate roles for industry, government, and universities. Industry through the AF&PA Agenda 2020 Technology Alliance is spearheading a drive to raise the visibility of nanotechnology in the forest products sector by (1) having a set of industry priority applications; (2) linking with the U.S. National Nanotechnology Initiative through a Forest Products Industry NNI-NILI-CBAN; (3) developing a core group of Federal laboratories, universities, and industry to advance an industry-led effort that makes use of the expertise that industry has to commercialize nanomaterials and nano-enabled products; and (4) identifying annual funding needs and funding sources.

Goal 2: Foster the transfer of new technologies into products for commercial and public benefit

The NNI member agencies have a number of activities uniquely targeting technology transfer and commercialization, e.g., workshops to gain input from industry and the academic community, SBIR and STTR programs to fund innovations in small businesses, and forefront research infrastructure for use by all nanotechnology researchers, including those from industry. Some positive results from this effort are now evident.

Individual Agency Contributions to Goal 2

DOD: Examples of emphasis and progress in DOD efforts within Goal 2 follow:

- A new detector imaging approach has been demonstrated that converts photons from an incoming optical signal into surface plasmon waves (as sound waves are produced by oscillating air molecules, plasmons are quantized oscillations of the electron gas in a metal). The plasmon waves are formed in a metal film that is typically less than 100 nm thick and bonded to a semiconductor substrate. The plasmon waves are collected by a slit in the metal film, where their energy is focused to produce electron/hole pairs in the semiconductor. The electron/hole pairs, in turn, give rise to a measurable electrical signal. Different polarization signals can be produced from the same imaging chip by fabricating different slit orientations, and multispectral signals can be produced by fabricating an imaging chip that has several different slit sizes. This accomplishment provides a decrease in detector size of at least 50% relative to existing technology at equivalent resolution.

- Munitions enhanced with nano-aluminum powder are being developed to give performance and lethality enhancements in miniaturized munitions needed for the reduced volume of advanced aircraft munitions bays and for weaponization of unmanned air vehicles (UAVs). Munitions using nano-aluminum powder may give improved lethality by improving the airblast and the shrapnel accelerating capability over conventional formulations. Nanoparticles have much higher surface area and are therefore more reactive for a given weight than conventional powders. The reaction rate of nanopowders can be controlled by adjusting the nanoparticle diameter, giving tailorability for optimized airblast and for fragment formation and acceleration. Only a few percent by volume of nano-aluminum powder could previously be added to munitions formulations, which created a barrier to the development, production, and characterization of advanced munitions with significant additions of nano-aluminum powders.

DOE: The Department of Energy supports nanotechnology transfer, industrial manufacturing activities, and commercialization through the Office of Energy Efficiency and Renewable Energy (EERE) and its Industrial Technologies Program (ITP). In 2011, ITP's Nanomanufacturing efforts will be focused on realizing the translation of the tremendous U.S. investment in nanoscience to the industrial sector through large-scale energy-efficient fabrication and functionalization of nanomaterials. This can only be achieved through the accelerated adaptation of advanced nanomanufacturing technologies developed through research, development, and deployment activities among national laboratories, universities, and industry. Examples of nanomaterial fabrication and functionalization technologies within ITP's portfolio include the following:

- Energy-efficient large-scale manufacturing of nanoparticles for photovoltaic and light-emitting diodes (LEDs)

- Nano-composite coatings for improved wear resistances, advanced lithium-ion battery electrodes, and dye-sensitized thin film photovoltaic applications

- Self-assembled, nanostructured carbon for energy storage and water treatment

- Nanocatalysts for diesel engine emission remediation and efficient biofuel production

DOT/FHWA: The Federal Highway Administration's Office of Research, Development, and Technology will maintain an increased investment in 2010 and 2011 through its Exploratory Advanced Research Program. Nanoscale approaches for inhibiting and mitigating corrosion and structural health monitoring via nanoscale sensors and devices are being pursued to enable more durable and efficient infrastructure systems.

NIH: Academic institutions involved in the National Cancer Institute's Alliance for Nanotechnology in Cancer have been very active in forming start-up companies dedicated to the clinical translation and commercialization of cancer diagnostics and therapeutics based on nanotechnology. Overall, 34 companies have been formed since the inception of the program (2005), and 250 patent disclosures have been issued or filed to cover intellectual property of these technologies.

The NIH also reissued the Bioengineering Nanotechnology Initiative for Small Business Innovation Research (PA-09-267) on October 2, 2009. The purpose of this trans-NIH solicitation is to stimulate Small Business Innovation Research that employs nanotechnology to enable the development of diagnostics and interventions for treating diseases. This FOA is designed to bring about fundamental changes to the diagnosis, treatment, and management of an array of diseases and traumatic injuries. To that end, the NIH has identified a wide range of research topics that focus on the engineering of nanoscale structures, processes, and systems as well as other technological innovations (data generation, research methods, etc.) to address biomedical challenges. In parallel, the NIH also reissued the Bioengineering Nanotechnology Initiative for Small Business Technology Transfer grant applications (PA-09-266) for the same purpose.

NIST: NIST's mission to develop measurement technologies in support of technology transfer includes significant nanotechnology investments. New examples include standard reference materials to enable nanoscale mapping of deformation, strain, and stress to ensure performance and mechanical reliability of products manufactured from nanostructured materials; and RM 8820, a new lithographically produced dimensional metrology calibration standard useful for calibrating scanning electron, scanning probe, and optical microscopes.

NRO: NRO-supported R&D for nanotechnology in electronics, structural materials, and power generation and energy storage devices pursues dual-use deliveries to entice commercial interest at the earliest stages. NRO transition goals aim to create commercial "pull" to enable rapid establishment of domestic 21st century manufacturing and to rapidly reduce product cost. CNT electronics developments are monitored by data storage vendors and data center manufacturers; the low-power-consumption and low-heat-production nature of CNT electronics will usher in a new paradigm for space and terrestrial data processing applications.

NSF: Ongoing and planned new activities in support of Goal 2 include the following:

- Strengthen the contribution of translational innovation programs from fundamental research, including in Grant Opportunities for Academic Liaison with Industry (GOALI), Partnerships for Innovation (PFI) , and Industry-University Cooperative Research Centers (IUCRC)
- Partnership with small businesses and large companies in the United States for projects on fundamental research with long-term goals of interest to industry
- Co-sponsor workshops on research directions together with industrial partners
- Increase focus on energy, cyber-physical systems, and synthetic biology research and education

Coordinated Activities with Other Agencies and Other Institutions Contributing to Goal 2

NNI member agencies and international standards bodies: Technical experts from multiple agencies, including DOD, DOE, EPA, NIOSH, NCI, NIST, and USDA/FS, are working to develop international documentary standards in nanotechnology through the International Organization for Standardization (ISO), as coordinated by the American National Standards Institute's U.S. Technical Advisory Group to ISO TC229 (Nanotechnologies). The Federal agencies' Interagency Committee on Standards Policy (ICSP), chaired by NIST, provides an additional forum for information exchange and coordination on standards policy issues relating to nanotechnology. NNI agencies are also participating in standards development activities within ASTM International's Committee E56 (Nanotechnology), the International Electrotechnical Commission Technical Committee 113 (Nanotechnology Standardization for Electrical and Electronics Products and Systems), and the Institute of Electrical and Electronics Engineers' Nanotechnology Council in developing nanotechnology-related documentary standards. This close cooperation with the American National Standards Institute helps NNI member agencies provide input reflecting U.S. priorities in the international standards arena.

NNI member agencies, OECD: The Department of State chaired the OECD Working Party on Nanotechnology (WPN) to advise on emerging policy issues in science, technology, and innovation related to the responsible development and use of nanotechnology. The WPN is assessing business environments, international research collaboration and coordination, available indicators and statistics, and approaches to public engagement.

NIH and IEEE: The NIH in conjunction with the IEEE Society sponsored a nanomedicine workshop in April 2009 that outlined ongoing research in nanotechnology and industrial applications of nanomedicine.

NIST, VAMAS: NIST led the establishment of the ten-nation Nanoparticle Populations Working Group in the Versailles Project on Advanced Materials and Standards (VAMAS). The group will develop an international consensus in measurement methods as a precursor to documentary standards development, with an initial focus on single-walled carbon nanotube chirality measurements.

NIST, NIH-NCI, FDA: These agencies are collaborating to develop reference materials and relevant measurement protocols for biomedical applications.

NRO, DOE, industry: 2011 will usher in CNT wire testing by Boeing, Tyco Electronics, Northrop Grumman, and Lockheed Martin. Oak Ridge National Laboratory has requested a 12-foot-long, one-inch-diameter cable for high voltage testing; such a cable offers an extraordinarily efficient means to transport power throughout the country.

NRO, A123 Systems: The carbon nanotube battery storage R&D team includes A123 Systems; success in CNT-based batteries offers a potential for 3-to 6-fold improvement in battery technology for electric cars and spacecraft.

NSF and other NNI agencies: The NSET Subcommittee's Nanomanufacturing, Industry Liaison, and Innovation (NILI) Working Group planned and conducted a workshop on Regional, State, and Local Initiatives in Nanotechnology on April 1–3, 2009. A report of the workshop is planned to be published in 2010.

NSF, NIST, and the semiconductor/electronics industry: NSF and NIST are continuing to work jointly with universities and a consortium of companies in the Semiconductor Industry Association (SIA) and the Semiconductor Research Corporation (SRC) on activities to support the Nanoelectronics Research Initiative (NRI) with the goal of demonstrating novel computing devices capable of replacing the complementary metal oxide semiconductor (CMOS) transistor as a logic switch in the 2020 timeframe. R&D activities are taking place at multi-university centers and at NSF nanoscience centers, including the Materials Research Science and Engineering Centers, Network for Computational Nanotechnology hubs, and Nanoscale Science and Engineering Centers (NSECs).

Goal 3: Develop and sustain educational resources, a skilled workforce, and the supporting infrastructure and tools to advance nanotechnology

Significant progress is being made on all three aspects of Goal 3. With respect to education and workforce development, education is among the chief objectives of NNI-funded university research. In addition, specific programs targeted at K–16 education, educating the public about nanotechnology, and improving nanotechnology curricula in U.S. schools and universities have been initiated and are growing in scale and reach. Details are provided in the following text. The extensive network of research centers, user facilities, and other infrastructure for nanotechnology research, which was a key element of the original NNI strategy, is now largely complete.[6]

Individual Agency Contributions to Goal 3

DOD: An instrument is being developed that combines the imaging capability of scanning probe microscopy with the nanomechanical measurement capabilities of instrumented indentation to create a capability to image variations of mechanical properties and topography within a test specimen. This tool will enable researchers to probe the mechanisms that determine responses of nanocomposites to stress at the appropriate length scales, ultimately guiding the design of more efficient structural composites for realistic naval applications.

FDA: In support of Goal 3, FDA plans to increase nanotechnology laboratory testing capacity at its campus in Maryland, and its National Center for Toxicological Research (NCTR)/Office of Regulatory Affairs (ORA) facility in Arkansas, to assess nanotechnology products and their safety. These resources will allow assessment and safety research in support of regulatory decision making. Top-tier priorities will consist of developing:

- Testing methods to assess the safety of products that use nanomaterials (including their stability and interaction with biological systems)

- Testing methods to assess the quality and effectiveness of products that use nanomaterials

- Standards to be incorporated in the preclinical safety assessment of products that contain nanomaterials

In addition, FDA will establish a scientific staff development and training program in nanotechnology. Nanotechnology is a multidisciplinary field requiring expertise in pharmacology, materials science, biology, physics, chemistry, medicine, and toxicology. With the funds requested, FDA will establish a program to train review staff to adequately evaluate the scientific data submitted in support of nanotechnology-containing product regulatory applications. This will include:

- Cooperative training and research work in nanotechnology at national laboratories, government-sponsored research centers, and the Nanotechnology Collaborative Opportunities for Research Excellence (CORE) grants program, described below in the subsection on Goal 4 coordinated activities

- Information exchange and coordination with international regulatory agencies to enable science-based harmonization and sharing of regulatory information and decision processes regarding nanotechnology

- Strengthening FDA nanotechnology scientific training and expertise

---

[6] See a detailed discussion of the U.S. NNI infrastructure in the *NNI Supplement to the President's FY 2008 Budget*, http://www.nano.gov/NNI_08Budget.pdf, including a map that shows the location of all the centers, networks, and user facilities (p. 21) and a list of participating academic institutions and national laboratories (pp. 29–33).

NIH: The National Cancer Institute's Alliance for Nanotechnology in Cancer issued administrative supplements to Cancer Nanotechnology Centers of Excellence under the ARRA totaling $4 million. The supplements will be used to maintain and enhance the student and post-doctoral workforce within the centers.

The Nanomedicine Common Fund Initiative includes a strong training component for graduate students and postdoctoral fellows through webinars, postdoctoral exchanges among labs, and trainee sessions at annual meetings. In addition, the NIH Office of the Director provided ARRA funding to support undergraduate and high school students to work in a nanomedicine laboratory and represent the University of California San Francisco at the International Genetically Engineered Machine (iGEM) competition.

In April 2009, NIH hosted NanoWeek, a unique series of events revolving around nanotechnology and its application to medicine and biomedical research. The events varied, with some broadcasted widely to educate the public about basic concepts and their potential applications to diagnosis and treatment of disease. Other events included scientific seminars, poster displays, and in-lab demonstrations of cutting-edge research in nanotechnology and nanomedicine geared to promote information exchange among scientists, clinicians, and engineers working in these disciplines.

NIST: The NanoFab, NIST's national nanofabrication and measurement facility, increased the number of research participants by 30% in the past year and plans to add over $5 million of new tools in 2010.

In 2009, NIST awarded ARRA-funded contracts totaling $6 million for nanomeasurement tools, and it plans to make additional such awards in 2010. Also using ARRA funds, NIST awarded $34.3 million in 2010 to support construction of nanoscience facilities at U.S. universities.

NSF: NSF plans to expand the outreach of the National Center for Nanotechnology Applications and Career Knowledge (NACK, main node at The Pennsylvania State University) to other educational clusters and states in the United States.

Coordinated Activities with Other Agencies and Institutions Contributing to Goal 3

DOD: The Aviation and Missile Research Development and Engineering Center is collaborating and leveraging multiple nanotechnology programs with the Oak Ridge National Laboratory (ORNL), Army Research Laboratory (ARL), and the Air Force Research Laboratory (AFRL) to broaden subject matter expertise and utilize specialized laboratories and equipment.

NIH, UC San Diego: The NCI is participating in webinars sponsored by the University of California San Diego. The aim of the webinars is to bring knowledge on medical nanotechnology to academics, physicians, and industrial researchers in the United States and abroad.

NIST, universities, industry: Through ARRA fellowship programs beginning in 2010, NIST will provide opportunities for students, faculty, and industrial researchers to interact with NIST scientists and conduct nanotechnology research in NIST laboratories

NIST, DOE: NIST state-of-the-art X-ray detectors, including an imaging microscope developed through the NIST SBIR program and procured with ARRA funds, have enabled NIST to expand its suite of world-class synchrotron instruments at the National Synchrotron Light Source at Brookhaven National Laboratory. These nanocharacterization instruments, accessible to the scientific community through the DOE User Program, have enabled collaborators from industry to develop advanced materials and devices, including next-generation catalysts.

NRO, national labs, universities, industry: The NRO nanotechnology R&D portfolio is aimed at rapidly developing and establishing a 21st century nanotechnology manufacturing base in the United States. The R&D team includes 22 companies, 2 Government labs, and 19 universities.

NSF, DOE, and DOD: NSF's Nanoscale Informal Science Education (NISE) Network and related projects will continue to provide shared knowledge, resources, and networking for educational activities with DOE and DOD in formal and informal settings.

NSF with DOE (Sandia National Laboratories), NIST, DOD, and NIH: These agencies are coordinating joint student fellowship programs in various areas of nanotechnology.

USDA/NIFA, DOE, and Canada: Following the successful joint grantees' meeting with Canada's Advanced Food and Materials Network (AFMNet) held in conjunction with the DOE Center for Integrated Nanotechnologies (CINT) Nanotechnology User Conference in September 2009 in Santa Fe, New Mexico, USDA/NIFA is planning for a Fall 2010 nanotechnology grantees' meeting with AFMNet and Canada's National Institute for Nanotechnology.

Goal 4: Support responsible development of nanotechnology

The NNI has made significant progress towards the goal of supporting responsible development of nanotechnology. Funding for nanotechnology-related EHS research continues to increase at a rate far in excess of the overall NNI budget growth rate, from $35 million in 2005 to $117 million in the 2011 request. This is only counting the narrowly defined *primary purpose* EHS R&D. The NNI agencies have reached a strong consensus on a comprehensive strategy to move these investments forward effectively, in line with the roles and responsibilities of the respective agencies involved. The NNI also maintains a strong portfolio of research on ethical, legal, and other societal implications of nanotechnology, along with support for innovative approaches to nanotechnology education at all levels, from K-12 though graduate education and public outreach.

Individual Agency Contributions to Goal 4

DOD: Although no major changes in DOD investment are expected among the four NNI goals, increased focus and coordination on responsible development of nanotechnology will continue to be a growing area of DOD emphasis as applications and manufacturing processes mature. Examples of emphasis and progress in DOD efforts within Goal 4 follow:

- Basic research has created a class of amplifying fluorescent polymers that detect hazardous substances with extremely high sensitivity. In the same research area, a family of nano-engineered, self-segregating additives has been developed that have the ability to transport active materials to the polymer/air interface to self-detoxify contaminated coatings.

- Nanoscale platforms are being developed to enable DNA cloning without the use of cells. A related program uses nanoscale polymerase chain reaction (nano-PCR) with a focus on ultrasensitive, rapid, high-fidelity identification of natural or genetically engineered pathogen strains. These programs will have sensitivities three orders of magnitude better than conventional PCR, permitting single-molecule amplification from complex, for instance, "dirty," environmental samples.

EPA: In support of its Nanomaterial Research Strategy, EPA has initiated a research program to understand which nanomaterials are most likely to enter the environment and how they move and transform within environmental media. This information will help the agency focus its human health and ecological effects research on those nanomaterials and pathways with the most potential for harmful human exposure. The program continues to generate results. For example, STAR researchers at Carnegie Mellon University modified iron oxide nanoparticles to enable them to quickly and easily clean up trichloroethylene, a common groundwater contaminant. Using various cellular models, researchers in EPA's own laboratories have examined the *in vitro* pulmonary toxicity of carbon nanotubes as well as the neurological toxicity of nanoscale titanium dioxide.

FDA: The emerging nature of the science and the potential for rapid development of applications for FDA-regulated products highlights the need for timely development of transparent, consistent, and sound regulatory and scientific evaluation pathways. For 2009, 2010, and 2011, FDA is conducting activities that support the following FDA-wide priorities: (1) build laboratory and product testing capacity, (2) enable scientific staff development and training, and (3) engage in collaborative and interdisciplinary research to address product characterization and safety. Together, these priorities will better enable FDA to support the responsible development of nanotechnology.

NIH/NIEHS: NIEHS has assembled a network of extramural researchers to identify reliable and reproducible assays and methods to assess the biological response to and potential hazard of nanomaterials. Assays under consideration include analysis of cellular functions, immunotoxicity, and genotoxicity. Other projects will examine the utility of proteomics and other data-intensive assays in assessing biological behavior of nanomaterials.

NIOSH: NIOSH received an increase in funding for 2010 in nanotechnology-related environmental, health, and safety research (PCA 7 and Goal 4) as a result of specific language included in the President's Supplemental Budget Request. These funds will provide direct support to an increase in NIOSH's investigations specific to evaluating the potential hazards of select nanomaterials, assessing human exposures in workplaces and associated potential health risks, evaluating controls and risk management practices for safe handling of nanomaterials, and developing guidance on medical screening and evaluation of workers. Specifically, NIOSH will accelerate its activities in the area of risk assessment for carbon nanotubes; develop improved methods to detect and measure select nanomaterials that are being commercialized in high volume, such as nanotubes and metal oxides; evaluate the effectiveness of respiratory protection; and begin to quantitatively evaluate engineering controls for the mitigation of human exposures and environmental releases.

NIST: NIST is developing measurement protocols and analysis methods needed to assess airborne nanoparticle concentrations and exposures. This work will support efforts to measure airborne levels of nanoparticles in research settings for use in safety evaluations as well as in studies of consumer products that may release nanoparticles into the air.

NIST is developing measurement methodologies and associated models for determining dynamic physico-chemical and toxicological properties of key nanomaterials in relevant media (e.g., air, water, soil, and biological matrices) and in release of these nanomaterials during manufacturing processes and from products throughout full product life cycles. Dynamic physico-chemical property measurements of nanomaterials will focus on changes in nanomaterial surface attributes (area, composition, morphology, and charge), transformation processes (e.g., aggregation, dissolution, electron transfer), transport, and fate. Toxicological property measurements will focus on genotoxicity and mechanistic cytotoxicity assays, as indicated by biomarkers and other indicators of toxicological response.

In 2010 and 2011 NIST plans to release important reference materials needed for uniform assessment of nanomaterials EHS, including carbon nanotubes and titanium dioxide nanoparticles.

NRO: Nanotechnology R&D in electronics, structural materials, and power generation and energy storage devices are conducted in plants complying with current EPA regulations. Researchers are working with the EPA to help establish improved procedures and rules to protect the health of workers handling nanotechnology substances.

NSF: New efforts by NSF toward Goal 4 are to focus on implications of the next generations of nanotechnology products and productive processes, as well as public participation in nanotechnology-related activities, at the NSECs on societal dimensions at Arizona State University and the University of California Santa Barbara.

USDA/NIFA: The NIFA Nanoscale Science and Engineering for Agriculture and Food Program (within AFRI) supports competitive grants to assess and analyze the perceptions and acceptance of nanotechnology applications to food and agriculture and nanotechnology-based products by the general public, agriculture producers and processing industry, and other stakeholders, using appropriate social science tools. This effort started in 2008 and has funded three projects. One of them was awarded to Cornell University, which has produced six "radio blast" pieces for the EarthSky program through interviewing experts about nanotechnology applications and implications for agriculture and food systems. The program is estimated to reach audiences of more than 14 million in the United States and other countries. Another grant funded a research project at the Michigan State University to address public perceptions of emerging applications of nanotechnologies in food and agricultural production, titled "Public Perceptions of Agrifood Nanotechnologies: Using Extension to Assess and Link Stakeholder Knowledge with Public Policies." The project seeks to develop within the Cooperative Extension System the capacity to train extension educators on (1) what nanotechnologies are and what their current and emerging applications are throughout the agrifood system, so that extension agents can speak knowledgeably about these matters with their clientele; and (2) develop in the agents the social science research skills for documenting key public perceptions as revealed through extension agent-client interaction, and for translating/transferring this information to agrifood policy organizations through delivery systems that increase the likelihood of the information being used. The long-term goal of this project is to inform and enhance socially responsive policies for agrifood nanotechnologies at national, state, and population-specific levels.

Coordinated Activities with other Agencies and Institutions Contributing to Goal 4

NNI member agencies, OECD: The DOS has chaired the OECD WPN to advise on emerging policy issues in science, technology, and innovation related to the responsible development and use of nanotechnology. EPA has chaired the OECD Working Party on Manufactured Nanomaterials (WPMN), which is leading an international effort by the 30 OECD member nations and other nonmember nations and organizations to coordinate and collaborate on approaches for better understanding the environmental, health, and safety impacts and the benefits of nanotechnology. In 2008, the WPMN embarked on a cooperative international program to conduct testing on 14 nanomaterials types across 59 environmental endpoints. The EPA is leading the U.S. effort to sponsor the testing of many of these materials.

CPSC, NIOSH, EPA: In 2010, CPSC will establish interagency agreements with NIOSH and EPA to complete a literature search and develop experimental procedures using scientifically credible protocols to quantify releases of and consumer exposures to nanosilver in treated consumer products. Special emphasis will be placed on exposures to young children.

CPSC, EPA, NIEHS, NIST, NNI, NIOSH: The NNI held 3 workshops in calendar year 2009 to review and update the critical research needs that are explicated in the NNI Strategy for Nanotechnology-Related

Environmental, Health, and Safety research. In February, NIOSH led a workshop focusing on human and environmental exposure assessment research needs, hosted by CPSC. NIST and EPA led the October workshop on nanomaterials in the environment and related instrumentation, metrology, and analytical methods needs. NIEHS and NIST led the November workshop on research to understand human health implications and the instrumentation, metrology, and analytical methods needed to achieve that understanding. The workshops were planned by representatives of industry, academia, the public health sector, and government. Nearly 200 people participated in each workshop. The results of the workshops will be compiled into reports that will inform the next iteration of the NNI EHS strategy. (For more details on these workshops see http://www.nano.gov/html/meetings/humanhealth/Series.html.)

DOD: The Army Missile Research, Development, and Engineering Center is currently collaborating with the Missile Defense Agency (MDA) on multiple efforts for weaponry safety and insensitive munitions utilizing nanomaterial-based propellants and developing radiation and temperature nanosensors that offer high performance in extremely harsh environments. AMRDEC is also collaborating with MDA on research for weaponry life extension by developing carbon-fiber composites based on a nanoparticle polymer system in which self-healing and morphing properties restore damaged surfaces to their original condition.

EPA, NSF, USDA/NIFA, EC: EPA's National Center for Environmental Research (NCER), the National Science Foundation, and USDA's NIFA will make awards in 2010 through a joint solicitation entitled, "Increasing Scientific Data on the Fate, Transport, and Behavior of Engineered Nanomaterials in Selected Environmental and Biological Matrices." This solicitation is a collaborative effort with the European Commission. The total estimated U.S. award amount is approximately $4.2 million.

EPA, NSF, NIH/NIEHS, NIOSH, and DOE: Since 2004 EPA's STAR grants program has coordinated interagency requests for applications; agencies involved have included NSF, NIEHS, NIOSH, and DOE. The fourth joint research solicitation by EPA's STAR program was issued in 2007. The solicitation was a collaboration between EPA, NSF, and DOE; over 130 research proposals were received. EPA awarded 15 grants, NSF awarded 6 grants, and DOE awarded 1 grant and made several awards to DOE laboratories. Individual grant awards totaled approximately $9 million. In addition, EPA recently awarded $2 million to study fate and transport in biological systems as part of an NIEHS-led request for applications.

EPA, NSF, NIH/NIEHS, NIOSH, USDA/NIFA, and EC: EPA is leading another interagency solicitation with NSF, NIH/NIEHS, NIOSH, and USDA/NIFA, all in coordination with the European Commission, focused on exposure and safety research data for engineered nanomaterials.

EPA, United Kingdom: EPA's NCER under its STAR research program will also fund two research "e-consortia" teams, each at $2 million for a 4-year period, in collaboration with two research consortia teams from the United Kingdom, on the topics, "Consortium for Manufactured Nanomaterial Bioavailability & Environmental Exposure" and "Transatlantic Initiative for Nanotechnology and the Environment."

FDA, other agencies, and universities: There are many classes of products where the FDA is currently the only agency to conduct research essential for science-based safety and/or risk assessments. While the agency can undertake some self-initiated research, the scale and range of issues and expertise involved necessitate collaborations with academic and government laboratories. Therefore, FDA will establish a CORE program to foster collaborative and interdisciplinary research addressing product characterization and safety. The nanotechnology CORE program will support peer-reviewed research at FDA and in collaboration with academia through grant mechanisms or other approaches. The CORE program will focus on:

- Measurement and detection methods for nanomaterials in FDA-regulated products
- Effects of specific nanomaterial characteristics, such as surface charge, shape, size, and composition, on particle behavior (e.g., distribution in the body) and biological outcomes (e.g., both beneficial effects and toxicities)
- Strategies to better predict, assess, and mitigate potential human health risks

NIH/NIEHS, NIST, NIH/NCI, FDA, NIOSH, Oregon Nanoscience and Microtechnologies Institute, and ASTM International: The NIH/NIEHS in collaboration with NIST held a workshop on Enabling Standards for Nanomaterial Characterization on October 8–9, 2008. The goal was to address the urgent need to accelerate standards development at the pre-standards stage. Sponsors and contributors include the National Cancer Institute, National Institute of Standards and Technology, U.S. Food and Drug Administration, Nanotechnology Characterization Laboratory at NCI-Frederick, National Institute of Occupational Safety and Health, Oregon Nanoscience and Microtechnologies Institute, and ASTM International.

NIH/NCI, NIH/NIEHS, NIH/NIBIB, and NIST: NIH/NCI and NIEHS held a one-day workshop at NIST on October 10, 2008, to establish an International Collaboration for NanoEHS Informatics aimed at developing a federated database system. The Collaboration seeks to establish a global resource of knowledge on nanomaterial characteristics and their biological interactions that can be systematically queried from multiple sites within an interoperable, federated system of databases. Follow-up discussions between NIBIB and NIEHS are underway to define possible venues to address these and related nanobioinformatic needs of the community (NanoHealth Enterprise).

NIH/NIEHS, EPA, and University of Massachusetts: These institutions and other academicians co-sponsored the International Conference on the Environmental Implications and Applications of Nanotechnology in June 2009 in Amherst, MA. The conference aim was to provide a valuable forum for scientists, regulators, and policymakers from academia, government, and industry to interact and share new knowledge on the health and environmental impacts of nanotechnology, green nanotechnology, and new environmental applications, and to help direct future research and regulatory needs. The conference discussed global health and safety issues surrounding engineered nanoparticles and nanotechnologies, especially in connection with occupational and environmental health, and provided insights into the latest research results and actions to assure the safety and thereby the future success of nanotechnologies.

NIH, Peoples Republic of China: International coordination of materials characterization and its standardization was a subject of a discussion at the "First Joint U.S.-China Symposium on Nanobiology and Nanomedicine" in Beijing, Peoples Republic of China, October 20–22, 2008 (see p. 31 for additional details).

NIOSH, all other NEHI member agencies: NIOSH led the organizing committee within the Nanotechnology Environmental and Health Implications Working Group to organize the NNI Health and Environmental Exposure Assessment workshop that took place February 24–25, 2009. The workshop aimed to provide an open forum to facilitate effective communication among stakeholders about progress achieved in the human and environmental exposure assessment research category and about the path forward for addressing research needs in this category.

NIOSH, OECD: NIOSH will continue its leadership role in the OECD WPMN steering group on Cooperation on Exposure Measurement and Exposure Mitigation. Within this activity NIOSH is leading the development of globally harmonized protocols for nanomaterial emission assessment, guidance for the use of personal protective equipment, and guidance for the use of engineering controls. NIOSH will also continue conducting experiments and contributing data for carbon nanotubes and nanostructured titanium dioxide (TiO_2), silver (Ag), and cerium dioxide (CeO_2) to the OECD WPMN sponsorship program for safety testing of nanomaterials.

NIOSH, World Health Organization (WHO): NIOSH will continue developing and disseminating best practices globally for working with nanomaterials in collaborations with occupational safety and health institutions and coordinating activities led by WHO collaborating centers in the nanotechnology area.

NIOSH, International Alliance for NanoEHS Harmonization (IANH): NIOSH will participate in the IANH round-robin testing of toxicological techniques to ensure their reproducibility and to facilitate development of globally harmonized approaches to safety testing.

NIOSH, ICON: NIOSH will continue active participation in the International Council on Nanotechnology's "Nano Good Practices Wiki" project, which aims to develop and maintain global best occupational practices for the safe handling of nanomaterials, utilizing a collaborative wiki software platform.

NIOSH, CPSC: Under an interagency agreement signed in 2008, NIOSH collaborates with the Consumer Product Safety Commission on studying exposure potential resulting from use of selected spray applications utilizing nanomaterials.

NIOSH, CPSC: In 2010, under an IAG between CPSC and NIOSH, NIOSH will conduct testing to determine the exposure impact of bathroom spray that contains engineered nanomaterials.

NIST, DOD: NIST and the U.S. Army Corps of Engineers co-organized a nanosilver workshop in March 2009 to identify the most pressing measurements and standards needs, including the selection of potential forms of nanosilver for international interlaboratory studies on nanosilver properties and stability.

NIST, CPSC: NIST is leading a coordinated research program with the Consumer Product Safety Commission to determine the release of nanoparticle flame retardants from fabrics and foams.

NIST, FDA, and EPA: These agencies are coordinating the development of benchmark data, measurement methods, and prototype reference materials for nanosilver for biomedical applications, including EHS assessments.

NSF, EPA: To ensure that nanotechnology is developed in a responsible manner, the National Science Foundation and the Environmental Protection Agency continue to fund (over five years, starting in September 2008) two Centers for the Environmental Implications of Nanotechnology (CEIN). The CEINs are an important addition to the NNI and will build on NSF's Center for Biological and Environmental Technologies (CBET) and EPA's STAR grants on nanotechnology. Led by the University of California Los Angeles and Duke University, the CEINs will study how nanomaterials interact with the environment and human health, resulting in better risk assessment and risk mitigation strategies. Each center works as a network, connected to multiple research organizations, industry, and government agencies, and emphasizes interdisciplinary research and education.

External Reviews of the NNI

Public Law 108-153 calls for periodic external reviews of the NNI by the National Nanotechnology Advisory Panel and by the National Research Council (NRC) of the National Academies.

Review by the President's Council of Advisors on Science and Technology, Designated as the National Nanotechnology Advisory Panel (PCAST/NNAP)

The most recent review of the NNI by the PCAST/NNAP was released in April 2008 (available online at http://www.whitehouse.gov/sites/default/files/microsites/ostp/PCAST-NNAP-NNI-Assessment-2008.pdf). The following is a list of the recommendations of this report, and the NNI responses to each of them:

1. Infrastructure, Management, and Coordination

- *1.1. **Ensure continuing support from NNI member agencies and from Congress for NNI multidisciplinary centers, networks, and user facilities for nanoscale research.** The NNI infrastructure of user facilities, centers, and networks is an unparalleled resource for the nanotechnology R&D community, but it requires sufficient funding to maintain and operate. Having had the foresight to establish these centers, DOE, NSF, NIH, and NIST should provide ongoing strong support for these vital assets. In particular, NSF and NIH should continue to fund large centers and collaborative research groups that enable the multidisciplinary approaches that are essential to advances in basic nanotechnology research. Such multidisciplinary research remains especially vital because many applications will emerge from research at the convergence of historically disparate fields of science and technology. The NNI should continue to foster both "curiosity-driven" researchers and "applications-driven" developers, and their interaction. [pp. 31–32]*

  - The funding for PCA 6 on major research facilities and instrumentation acquisition has remained steady over the last seven years with a small increase in 2010. However, contrary to this recommendation, some agencies are not sustaining all of their investments in multidisciplinary research centers. For example, several directorates at NSF are de-emphasizing support for NSF's Nanoscale Science and Engineering Centers, and NSF has discontinued support for its Nanoscale Interdisciplinary Research Team (NIRT) awards.

  - NHLBI and NCI have released solicitations to renew their multidisciplinary centers in 2010 funded through the Programs of Excellence in Nanotechnology and Cancer Centers of Nanotechnology Excellence programs, respectively. NIH also continues to support large multidisciplinary research groups under the Nanomedicine Common Fund Initiative, and the Bioengineering Research Partnerships, several of which are in the nanotechnology area.

  - ARRA funding made available in 2009 has been used in part to upgrade equipment at NSF and DOE user facilities.

  - NNI "signature initiatives" proposed for 2011 and beyond (see sidebar at the end of Section 1 of this document) will help improve the balance between "curiosity-driven" and "applications-driven" research funded under the NNI auspices.

- *1.2. **Seek to improve intra-agency coordination.** Due to the scope and breadth of nanotechnology's impact, the NNAP recommends that each department and agency with numerous operating divisions impacted by nanotechnology (including DOC, DOD, EPA, HHS, and USDA) establish a cross-cutting task force or some similar mechanism to coordinate and optimize nanotechnology activities and policies more uniformly within the agency as a whole. Where such groups already exist, they should be supported at all levels and should be strengthened horizontally and vertically within the agency. The FDA's Nanotechnology Task*

Force, which incorporates representation from each of its centers, is a notable example. These intra-agency groups, which should include policy, communications, and budget specialists, will foster improved communication within the agency, across the Federal Government, and with outside stakeholders and agency customers. [p. 32]

- In addition to FDA, agencies with active internal nanotechnology coordinating groups that have been reported are DOD, EPA, NIH, and NSF.

- The NNCO and the NSET Subcommittee have also been strongly encouraging agencies to establish nanotechnology portal websites that point to all nanotechnology-related activities within the respective agencies. Agencies with nanotechnology portal websites include DOE, EPA, FDA, NASA, NIBIB, NIOSH, NIST, NSF, OSHA, and USDA/NIFA. The NNI website (http://www.nano.gov; see About the NNI/Departments and Agencies) points to the portal websites that have been established or to the agency's homepage where there is no nanotechnology portal page yet.

- *1.3. Strengthen participation in the NNI by DOC (beyond NIST), DOEd, and DOL in light of their respective departmental missions. Interdisciplinary training, broad-based education, workforce preparation, market assessment and evaluation, and standards development are critical challenges for nanotechnology and are essential for the United States to achieve the expected societal and economic benefits of nanotechnology research, development, and commercialization. These needs warrant closer involvement from these agencies in the NNI than has existed to date.* [p. 32]

  - Work continues on broadening participation from the agencies PCAST identified, but their participation has already expanded. Within DOC, the NSET Subcommittee and its working groups have had active participants from the Economics and Statistics Administration, the Bureau of Industry and Security (covering export control issues), and the International Trade Administration, in addition to NIST's strong participation. The subcommittee also includes active representation from the Department of Education, which played a strong role in the April 2009 NNI Workshop on Regional, State, and Local Nanotechnology Initiatives, and which with NSF co-sponsored a workshop on nanotechnology education in 2009. The Department of Education has one active representative, and the Department of Labor has designated two staff members as participants in the NSET Subcommittee.

- *1.4. Coordinate NSET Subcommittee and working groups activities more broadly with related NSTC interagency working groups, especially the Interagency Working Group on Manufacturing R&D, which has identified nanomanufacturing as an area of opportunity.* [p. 32]

  - Before this 2008 PCAST report was prepared, the Manufacturing R&D Interagency Working Group co-sponsored a workshop on instrumentation, metrology, and standards for nanomanufacturing, in collaboration with the NSET Subcommittee, NIST, NSF, and ONR. OSTP is currently evaluating ways to better support advanced manufacturing (including nanomanufacturing) and has convened representatives from multiple agencies and interagency working groups (including the NSET Subcommittee) to strengthen coordination and initiate interagency strategy development.

  - The NSET Subcommittee and NNCO have coordinated closely with the Multi-Agency Tissue Engineering Science (MATES) Interagency Working Group (IWG). IWG members assisted in organizing an NNI workshop on nanobiotechnology, for example. During 2009, the NSET

Subcommittee and NNCO worked with MATES IWG members in the development of an NNI Signature Initiative proposal on nanotechnology for regenerating the human body.

- NNCO and the National Coordination Office for Networking and Information Technology R&D (NCO/NITRD) are co-located; staff members confer on matters of mutual interest on a regular basis. There has also been a series of meetings to discuss the intersection between the NNI and NITRD, particularly with respect to quantum information science.

- The chair of the new NSTC Subcommittee on Quantum Information Science (SQIS) has met with NCO and NNCO staff several times to discuss the intersections between the three groups. The SQIS chair assisted in editing the QIS portion of the proposal for an NNI Signature Initiative on Nanoelectronics for 2020 and Beyond (see the sidebar at the end of Section 1).

- **1.5. Continue to function as the central coordination structure for nanotechnology R&D—including nanotechnology EHS research.** *The NSET Subcommittee, its working groups, and the NNCO have been, and should continue to be, the locus of coordination for all nanotechnology-related activities. Congress, to the extent that it engages these issues, should support the current interagency coordination and management structure of the NNI through the NSET Subcommittee and the NNCO.* [p. 32]

  - The NSET Subcommittee and the NNCO have continued to serve this function, as recommended. For example, as discussed in detail earlier in this document, the NSET Subcommittee has funded, and the NEHI Working Group has organized, a series of NNI workshops in 2009 and 2010 to gather community and stakeholder input on the evolving NNI strategy for nanotechnology-related EHS research. Additional workshops are planned for 2010 to gather input for the next update of the overall NNI Strategic Plan, due to be completed in December 2010.

2. Standards Development

- **2.1. Participate in the development of voluntary consensus-based standards,** *which are crucial to research, commercialization, and safe handling and use of nanotechnology. The NNI agencies, individually and jointly through the NNCO, should participate in and support standards development activities. In particular, the NNI should support U.S. participation at key international standards bodies, such as the International Organization for Standards (ISO). Through Federal agency participation, the NNI should seek to avoid duplication of standards development work at organizations that have overlapping areas of activity.* [p. 32]

  - Before this PCAST report was written, the funding agencies of the NSET Subcommittee voted explicitly not to continue to sponsor U.S. participation in ISO TC-229 ("Nanotechnologies") through NNCO financial contributions to ANSI (the only U.S. accredited representative at ISO). NNCO did provide some support for the ANSI TAG to ISO TC-229 in the first two years of its existence, but that support was discontinued at the end of 2007. Instead, the NSET Subcommittee members feel that ANSI should request this support directly from each of the member agencies. ANSI has done so, with mixed results so far. However, the subcommittee is supporting, particularly through travel funding, the extensive activities of the NNCO Director as chair of the ANSI TAG to ISO TC-229.

  - In a similar vein, the NSET Subcommittee provided $125,000 of seed funding to OECD to support the establishment of its Working Party on Nanotechnology (WPN), which is addressing a broad range of economic development issues associated with nanotechnology. EPA has also supported the OECD Working Party on Manufactured Nanomaterials (WPMN), which is addressing EHS issues associated with nanotechnology. The subcommittee's support for the WPN was only a one-time arrangement to help start up the WPN. However, it continues to provide support for NNCO staff to attend WPN meetings.

- Reports on ISO and OECD nanotechnology-related activities are scheduled as regular agenda items at NEHI and GIN working group meetings.

- *2.2. Develop materials and analytical standards for nanotechnology EHS research. Such standards are critical to characterizing and monitoring effects of nanomaterials. NIST should lead the development work, in consultation and collaboration with agencies that use such standards, including EPA and FDA. The initial focus should be on nanomaterials that have or are moving toward broad commercial use (e.g., nanoscale gold, silver, metal oxides, carbon nanotubes, and other materials such as those identified in the OECD list of fourteen most common nanomaterials in current applications). [p. 32]*

  - The NSET Subcommittee collaborated with NIST in organizing a Workshop on Material Standards for Environmental Health & Safety for Engineered Nanoscale Materials (Sept. 2007, just as this PCAST report was being prepared). NNCO has been assisting NIST in preparing the report from that workshop for publication.

  - As recommended above, NIST has taken the lead in developing standard reference materials for a number of nanomaterials now entering commerce, e.g., gold nanoparticles and carbon nanotubes. NIST has worked closely with NIH/NCI, EPA, and FDA in developing these materials.

- *2.3. Work towards development of minimum data sets of physical and chemical properties of nanomaterials. If properly defined, adoption of a minimum set of data for research on nanomaterials would ensure accurate communication of research results and product properties. It would also enable comparison and reproducibility of EHS testing. This is essential to ensure that evaluations are meaningful and that the assessments of potential EHS impacts are sound. NIST should take a leading role in coordinating efforts to this end among the interagency NNI members. [p. 33]*

For clarity, the following response pertains to efforts by the NNI member agencies to work with the ISO Technical Committee 229 on Nanotechnologies, the OECD Working Party on Manufactured Nanomaterials, and the broad EHS research community to come to agreement on a minimum set of parameters/properties of nanomaterials for proper characterization of nanomaterials before use in toxicological research studies. Without such proper characterization, many early studies of the toxicological properties of nanomaterials have led to completely wrong conclusions and inferences.

- This continues to be a critical and largely unmet need. Scientific reviewers and journal editors have been particularly reluctant to require such baseline characterizations as a condition for publication, fostering an avalanche of one-off, non-reproducible studies that offer little clarity on nanomaterial EHS implications nor an adequate basis for regulatory decision making.

- NNI member agencies and the NNCO continue to support work at OECD's WPMN and at ISO Technical Committee on Nanotechnologies' working group on EHS aspects of nanotechnologies to develop such a minimum set of characterization parameters of materials properties for purposes of EHS testing.

- The OECD WPMN is now using a generally agreed upon set of 9 nanomaterials properties for characterizing 14 nanomaterials in relatively common commercial use. ISO TC 229 Working Group 3 also is nearing completion of a Technical Report recommending a similar set of 9 properties for characterization of nanomaterials for toxicological studies.

3. Technology Transfer and Commercialization

- ***3.1. Expand efforts to assess national and international innovation and commercialization activities.*** *While the NNAP commends current and ongoing efforts, the NNI—led by DOC—should identify metrics and obtain data that will allow accurate assessment of the economic impact of nanotechnology development. This will require closer and more coordinated involvement from DOC and continued engagement with OECD to obtain better data at the national and international levels. The downstream impact of nanotechnology development on the economy remains difficult to quantitatively assess, but market projections based on well-defined categories of nanomaterials and devices and specific classes of products will allow for some reasonable estimates, if properly qualified. In any case, since so many industries are involved in nanotechnology development, it appears clear that nanotechnology will have a large economic impact, and continuously monitoring that impact is an important role DOC should play.* [p. 33]

  - The NSET Subcommittee's support for OECD/WPN discussed above was motivated by the need to expand our understanding of international innovation and commercialization activities. Some preliminary reports from WPN are now becoming available. A representative from the DOC Economic Statistics Administration was initially an active participant in the WPN, and representatives from the DOC International Trade Administration have been engaged in the NSET Global Issues in Nanotechnology working group since 2009.

  - NSF has funded a group at the Georgia Institute of Technology to gather information and analyze trends in commercialization of nanotechnology. NSF has also sponsored the National Center for Manufacturing Sciences (NCMS) to gather information on nanotechnology companies in the United States.

  - NNCO has just concluded an arrangement with Lux Research to provide NSET Subcommittee members with access to Lux's data on nanotechnology companies and related information on economic impact and commercialization.

  - NNCO also funds the Asian Technology Information Program (ATIP) to gather information on nanotechnology R&D and commercialization activities in Asia.

  - NSF has just initiated a World Technology Evaluation Center (WTEC) international benchmarking study on nanotechnology. Several other NSET Subcommittee member agencies may also contribute to the study. Preliminary results from the study should be available in late 2010.

- ***3.2. Continue to build connections across the innovation ecosystem,*** *including requiring that multidisciplinary centers partner with industry or with economic development organizations. NSF, NIH, and other major supporters of multidisciplinary nanotechnology-focused centers should explicitly support, maintain, and strengthen cross-sector linkages.* [p. 33]

  - As documented elsewhere in this report, NNI agencies have strong collaborations with several key industries that view nanotechnology as key to their future, including the semiconductor industry, the chemical industry, and the forest products industry. Efforts to establish similar connections with other industries are continuing.

  - Agencies have required that proposals for interdisciplinary research centers funded under the NNI demonstrate strong industry partnerships. For example, NCI Alliance for Nanotechnology in Cancer centers have been required since their inception in 2005 to collaborate with industry. The centers, based at universities, have been very active in forming start-up companies dedicated to the clinical translation and commercialization of cancer diagnostics and therapeutics based on nanotechnology. Overall, 34 companies were formed since the inception of the program (2005), and 250 patent disclosures were issued or filed to cover intellectual property of these technologies.

- The NSET Subcommittee and several of its member agencies are continuing to sponsor technical workshops covering topics that are of interest across multiple industrial sectors. For example, in May 2008, NIST and USDA/FS sponsored an NNI-affiliated workshop on cross-industry issues in nanomanufacturing.

- The NSET working group on Nanomanufacturing, Industrial Liaison, and Innovation (NILI) continues its work reaching out to regional, state, and locally-based initiatives and to specific industry sectors, including electronics, chemicals, and forest products, through its Consultative Boards for Advancing Nanotechnology.

- **3.3. *Educate more scientists and engineers*** *to become entrepreneurs and skilled technology workers. Transfer of know-how and ideas from university labs to products and processes with commercial value and public benefit occurs primarily through college and university education and research activities. Funding world-class research is the best "training program" for top-notch nanoscale scientists and engineers. The NSF Integrative Graduate Education Research and Traineeship (IGERT) program is a notable model in this regard, particularly with respect to interdisciplinary nanotechnology training and R&D.* [p. 33]

  - Earlier sections of this report discuss a number of activities aimed at the issues discussed in this recommendation. See Section 4 of this report, particularly activities described there relating to Goal 2 (foster the transfer of new technologies into products for commercial and public benefit) and Goal 3 (develop and sustain educational resources, a skilled workforce, and the supporting infrastructure and tools to advance nanotechnology).

4. Environmental, Health, and Safety Implications

- **4.1. *Coordinate the nanotechnology EHS strategy with industry and international stakeholders.*** *EHS research is noncompetitive; therefore, the NNI should coordinate efforts in this area with the activities of industry and other countries so as to avoid duplication and to leverage investments. NNI member agencies should work centrally through the NNCO and/or consensus lead agencies designated in the NNI nanotechnology EHS research strategy to coordinate their respective research activities with other relevant entities.* [p. 33]

  - The current (2009/2010) NNI series of EHS workshops are specifically designed to engage stakeholders from all sectors, including industry and international organizations, to gather input on the U.S. strategy for nanotechnology-related EHS research and regulatory activities. The planning teams for each of the workshops conducted in late 2009 and early 2010 include equal participation from industry, non-governmental organizations, universities, and U.S. Government agencies.

  - The OECD/WPMN is aimed at improving international coordination in EHS research and policy development. For example, WPMN is organizing an international collaboration to conduct a series of standard characterization tests on nanomaterials currently in commerce or expected to be in commerce soon.

  - ISO TC-229 includes a Working Group 3 on EHS aspects of nanotechnology. This is another appropriate forum for coordinating EHS activities internationally.

- **4.2. Do not segregate implications research and applications research.** *In many instances, nanotechnology EHS research cannot be separated from the particular application(s) research and from the context for which a specific nanomaterial is intended. Such division is unproductive and neglects the whole benefit of research. Consequently, the NNAP expects that a substantial fraction of nanotechnology research related to EHS will continue to take place under the auspices of agencies that fund applications R&D and may not be uniquely or exclusively identified as nanotechnology EHS research. Risk research that is performed independent of applications development should nevertheless be carried out with consideration of overall risks and benefits associated with the particular material or technology. Furthermore, detailed reporting on the degree of relevance to EHS of such research is not necessarily critical to (and may actually hinder) overall prioritization and coordination.* [p. 34]

    - The NNI participating agencies have been criticized (e.g., from the most recent National Academies review of the NNI) for linking implications research to applications research. The December 2008 National Academies Board on Environmental Studies and Toxicology report dismissed a number of the EHS projects reported in the Feb. 2008 NNI EHS strategy document as "not explicitly associated with risk…" (p. 7) and also claimed that EHS research funding figures published by the NNI are overstated because they included projects not directly relevant to nanotoxicology. However, only a small proportion of the funding for NIH projects listed in the 2006 snapshot of NNI EHS projects (included as an appendix to the Feb. 2008 NNI EHS strategy document) was actually counted by the NNI as EHS funding; the remainder was reported in other PCAs appropriate to the health-related applications that those projects are targeting. This is precisely consistent with the 2008 PCAST report recommendation. Virtually every NIH health applications project includes as an integral component some research to make sure that the diagnostic and therapeutic applications being developed are not only effective but are also safe.

- **4.3. Continue developing joint programs among NNI agencies that leverage expertise and resources to conduct nanotechnology EHS research and to support agency missions.** *The NNI member agencies should proactively seek to collaborate on priority EHS research, where appropriate, in order to expedite progress and take advantage of competency and knowledge that is distributed across the Federal Government.* [p. 34]

    - The NNI participating agencies have collaborated on a number of joint interagency efforts to organize and fund EHS workshops listed under the Coordinated Activities section of Goal 4 in this report.

    - The NNI participating agencies have funded a series of joint interagency solicitations for nanotechnology-related EHS research in recent years. The agency participation and research foci of these solicitations continue to evolve. Examples include the NSF-EPA Centers for Environmental Implications of Nanotechnology.

- **4.4. Support wide distribution and availability of new nonproprietary information about the properties of nanomaterials.** *Such information should include methods for risk/benefit analysis that can be implemented by researchers, as well as by developers and manufacturers.* [p. 34]

    - NIST continues work assessing the physico-chemical properties of key nanomaterials and developing standard reference materials. NCI's Nanotechnology Characterization Laboratory (NCL) also provides this kind of information about nanomaterials being considered for use in clinical applications, with nearly 160 nanoparticles in its assay cascade of physical, *in vitro*, and *in vivo* characterization. (Data and recommended assays by material type are available at http://ncl.cancer.gov.) As indicated earlier, EPA continues its leadership of the international project in OECD's WPMN to develop a wide variety of characterizations of 14 nanomaterials in commercial use.

5. Societal and Ethical Implications

- *5.1. Research on the societal and ethical aspects of nanotechnology should both be integrated with technical R&D and take place in the context of broader societal and ethical scholarship. Societal research should continue to be addressed in conjunction with technical research activities. However, these discussions will also be advanced by involvement of researchers who are primarily engaged in social science, ethics of technology, and other members of the broader academic community with expertise on science, technology, and society. [p. 34]*

  - Some centers that NSF has funded to address societal and ethical implications of nanotechnology are co-located with major NNI-funded nanotechnology research centers. Social scientists and nanotechnologists are interacting closely in these centers.

  - The NNCO Director is leading the ISO TC229 Task Group on Consumer and Societal Dimensions of Nanotechnologies. The principal tasks assigned to this group are to explore how all the 32 member countries of the Technical Committee are integrating societal and consumer aspects of nanotechnology into their work on nanotechnology standards and to survey all the other ISO technical committees (some 200) to determine how they are integrating this topic into their standards efforts.

6. Communication and Outreach

- *6.1. Demonstrate more clearly to the public the value of nanotechnology and NNI-supported research and development. Broader communication and outreach efforts are an essential part of successful innovation. A lack of information and basic understanding of nanotechnology by the general public fosters susceptibility to exaggerated claims and to miscommunications that generate unfounded hopes or fears; these in turn may inhibit future nanotechnology innovation and societal benefit. While communication is a fundamental responsibility of all researchers, a number of specific NNI programs are pursuing efforts to address this both broadly (e.g., the NSF Nanoscale Informal Science Education Network, or NISE Net) and more narrowly, in areas of application (e.g., the model communications efforts of the Alliance for Nanotechnology in Cancer program at NCI). Nonetheless, the NNI should undertake a more explicit and direct outreach approach to better inform and engage policymakers, stakeholders of all types, and the general public in a dialog as to the application-specific status and associated risk-benefit ratio of relevant near-commercial and commercial nanotechnologies; and to convey the significance of nanotechnology-based capabilities to address grand challenges and future opportunities across industry sectors. Failing to effectively communicate the complete risk-benefit pictures with respect to various specific nanotechnology applications as they exist to date will hinder realization of the significant societal benefits, both demonstrated and promised, of nanotechnology advancements. [pp. 34–35]*

  - In addition to the various NSF-funded activities mentioned above, NNCO has undertaken a number of activities aimed at communicating better to the public, policymakers, and other stakeholders the potential of nanotechnology. A major redesign of the NNI website, http://www.nano.gov, is currently underway, including new sections to facilitate public outreach. A brochure on nanotechnology intended for general audiences was completed in 2007 and has been so popular (e.g., with requests for thousands of copies coming from public school systems) that it is now in its third printing—two printings of 10,000 each have been distributed. NNCO is developing a similar brochure discussing the potential of nanotechnology to improve energy conversion, storage, transmission, and efficient utilization. Other brochures on EHS and health applications are planned. The NNCO has a concerted effort underway to develop video footage about various aspects of nanotechnology that will be offered to local TV stations for their use in developing news stories about nanotechnology Finally, NNCO is now completing a first draft of a report documenting commercial spinoffs and research accomplishments arising from the NNI.

- *6.2. Enhance communications efforts within the NNCO. As an interagency office, the NNCO is well positioned to serve as a central point for much of the communication activity outlined above. In addition, the office also should coordinate among NNI agencies to enhance their agency-specific communication efforts. Member agencies should provide for greater resources to be directed toward these activities.* [p. 35]

  - The 2010 NNCO communications plan addresses this recommendation. At the recommendation of the NSET Subcommittee, NNCO staff now includes two full-time communications professionals. NNCO has been reaching out to communications and public affairs offices in the NNI participating agencies but has experienced some challenges in engaging these offices in many of the agencies.

7. Additional EHS Recommendations in the July 2008 PCAST/NNAP Addendum Report

The 2008 PCAST/NNAP report was almost completed when the NSET Subcommittee released its Strategy for Nanotechnology-Related Environmental, Health, and Safety Research in February 2008. Rather than delay the release of the NNAP report, PCAST issued an addendum to its report in July 2008 (http://www.whitehouse.gov/sites/default/files/microsites/ostp/PCAST-Addendum-Letter.pdf) explicitly reviewing the NNI EHS strategy document. The following is a list of the recommendations from that addendum, and the NNI responses to each of them:

- *7.1. Assess Federal nanotechnology EHS portfolio and update gap analysis against research priorities triennially* [p. 4]

  - As part of the process of evaluating and adaptively managing the Federal strategy for nanotechnology-related EHS research, the Office of Management and Budget will issue a new data call to identify and analyze 2009 nanotechnology-related EHS projects funded by NNI participating agencies.

  - As another integral part of this process, the NEHI Working Group, under the sponsorship of the NSET Subcommittee, has launched a series of four workshops treating the five EHS research areas identified in the 2008 Strategy for Nanotechnology-Related EHS Research. After the completion of the fourth workshop in March 2010, NEHI, through its task forces, will use the workshop proceedings to inform and make recommendations to the NSET Subcommittee for adaptively managing the Federal EHS strategy. The first three workshops, held in 2009, assembled experts from academia, state, Federal, and international governments, industry, stakeholders, and the general public to identify the state of the science, review and update the identified EHS research needs, and identify the barriers and gaps to achieving these prioritized research needs.

  - The goal is to release an updated EHS strategy document in late 2010 or early 2011, integrating input from both the updated data call and the workshops described above.

- *7.2. Leverage opportunities to bootstrap identified gap areas and to encourage increased investments elsewhere through collaboration with industry and other countries; encourage broad and ongoing agency participation in such efforts* [p. 4]

- NEHI Working Group member agencies regularly collaborate and coordinate their activities with each other and with other public and private entities, both nationally and internationally, as detailed elsewhere in this report. For example, EPA leads the U.S. delegation to the OECD's Working Party on Manufactured Nanomaterials, whose body of work includes testing 14 nanomaterials; DOS has chaired the OECD's Working Party on Nanotechnology; NIST is working with other agencies including EPA, FDA, NIOSH, NCI and DOD to develop international documentary standards in nanotechnology. NSF, EPA, and USDA are coordinating a joint solicitation with the European Commission to promote interagency and international collaboration on EHS research.

- **7.3. Encourage supported researchers to report on the development of analytical methodologies used in their research so that a series of best practices can evolve for risk assessment and characterization** [p. 5]

  - NEHI Working Group member agencies are working together and with other organizations to develop the science and tools to support best practices. The two fall 2009 NNI workshops were deliberately cross-disciplinary efforts in part to identify critical instrumentation, metrology, and analytical methods needed to support best practices in EHS research for the environment and for human health. Presentations included expert comments on the scientific and technical challenges to creating reliable and reproducible best practices. Other examples include NIH/NCI and NIEHS holding a one-day workshop on nanoEHS informatics to provide a global resource of knowledge on nanomaterial characteristics and their biological interactions; NIH/NIEHS, NIST/NIH/NCI, FDA, NIOSH, Oregon Nanoscience and Microtechnologies Institute, ASTM International, and American National Standards Institute holding a workshop to accelerate standards development; NIOSH participating in the International Alliance for NanoEHS Harmonization round-robin testing of toxicological techniques to ensure their reproducibility and to facilitate the development of globally harmonized approaches to safety testing; and NIST and DOD jointly organizing a workshop on nanosilver to identify the most pressing standards and measurement needs.

- **7.4. Promote broad and practical use of EHS findings in defining responsible use of nanotechnology in research, manufacturing and commercial application** [p. 5]

  - Individual NEHI Working Group member agencies and interagency collaborations are promoting and putting into practice EHS findings. Examples include DOD research to create a class of polymers that detect hazardous substances, EPA's funding of research to use nanoparticles to quickly and easily clean up a groundwater contaminant, a boost in FDA funding to address the increase in numbers and complexity of products involving nanoscale materials under its review, and NSF efforts to focus on the implications for the next generation of nanotechnology and focusing on public participation. The fourth NNI EHS workshop in March 2010 will be on EHS risk management decision making to promote responsible product development while protecting public health. The workshop will also enlarge the EHS discussion to encompass the ethical, legal, and societal implications of nanotechnology.

- **7.5. Increase exposure assessment funding** [p. 5]

  - NIOSH is the agency whose research efforts are most closely associated with funding for exposure assessment. In 2009 the agency invested $6.7 million in EHS research, its 2010 budget is estimated to rise to $9.5 million, and it proposes $16.5 million for 2011, a two-and-a-half–fold increase over 2009. These funds will directly support NIOSH's investigations of the potential hazards of select nanomaterials, assessing human exposures in the workplace, evaluating controls and risk management practices for the safe handling of nanomaterials, and developing guidance on medical screening and evaluation of workers.

- ● **7.6. Maintain and strengthen agency support and coordination efforts through the NSET subcommittee and NEHI working group** [p. 5]

  - As indicated above, agencies are exhibiting strong coordination and collaboration through the NSET Subcommittee and the NEHI Working Group. Examples include the NSET Subcommittee retreat convened in June 2008 (and planned again for June 2010) and the Nanotechnology Signature Initiatives developed by the agency representatives and selected for support in the 2011 budget (including nanotechnology for electronics, solar energy, and sustainable manufacturing).

Review by the National Research Council of the National Academies

The last National Academies review of the NNI, *A Review of the Federal Strategy for Nanotechnology-Related Environmental, Health, and Safety Research* (http://www.nap.edu/catalog.php?record_id=12559), was released in February 2009. The following is a summary of the major findings and recommendations of this report, and the NNI responses to each of them:

Findings

- ● *The National Nanotechnology Initiative document* Strategy for Nanotechnology-Related Environmental, Health, and Safety Research *could be an effective tool for communicating the breadth of federally supported research associated with developing a more comprehensive understanding of the environmental, health, and safety implications of nanotechnology. It is the result of considerable collaboration and coordination among 18 federal agencies and is likely to eliminate unnecessary duplication of their research efforts.* [p. 93]

  - NNI representatives appreciate this recognition of some of the merits of the NNI strategy document.

- ● *The* Strategy for Nanotechnology-Related Environmental, Health, and Safety Research *does not describe a strategy for nano-risk research. It lacks input from a diverse stakeholder group, and it lacks essential elements, such as a vision and a clear set of objectives, a comprehensive assessment of the state of the science, a plan or road map that describes how research progress will be measured, and the estimated resources required to conduct such research.* [p. 93]

  - The members of the NEHI Working Group who prepared the February 2008 NNI Strategy for Nanotechnology-Related Environmental, Health, and Safety Research and the members of the NSET Subcommittee who reviewed and approved the document fully recognize the limitations of their first comprehensive Federal strategy for nanotechnology-related EHS research; this strategy explicitly calls for its continuous updating and improvement. However, NNI representatives challenge the factual underpinnings for some of the findings of this National Academies panel, including the bullet above summarizing a number of criticisms of the NNI strategy that appear throughout this National Academies report. The NNCO brought these factual issues to the attention of the National Academies staff after the release of the pre-publication version of this report in December 2008. The National Academies addressed some, but not the most substantive, of these issues in its final report, released in February 2009. Subsequently, with review and clearance from the Office of Science and Technology Policy, NNCO published a public rebuttal of some of the National Academies study findings, outlining the factual issues that had not been corrected in the final version of the report, many of which were the basis for major findings and recommendations. For full text of the January 5, 2009, NNI response to the factual misstatements in the NRC review, the reader is referred to the NNCO document on the NNI website, http://www.nano.gov/Response_to_NRC_Report_2_13_09.pdf.

Recommendations

- *There remains an urgent need for the nation to build on the current research base related to the EHS implications of nanotechnology—including the federally supported research described in the 2008 NNI document—by developing a national strategic plan for nanotechnology- related environmental, health, and safety research.* [p. 93; another boldface section on p. 97 outlines what this plan should include]

  - EPA recently funded the Board on Environmental Studies and Toxicology (BEST) at the National Academies to develop a national implementation plan or roadmap for nanotechnology-related EHS research that builds on the NNI EHS research strategy. It is expected to engage both public and private stakeholders, identifying roles and responsibilities as well as requisite resources.

- *As part of a broader strategic plan, NNI should continue to foster the successful interagency coordination effort that led to its 2008 document with the aim of ensuring that the federal plan is an integral part of the broader national strategic plan for investments in nanotechnology-related environmental, health, and safety research. In doing so, it will need a more robust gap analysis. The federal plan should identify milestones and mechanisms to ascertain progress and identify investment strategies for each agency. Such a federal plan could feed into a national strategic plan but would not itself be a broad, multistakeholder national strategic plan. Development of a national strategic plan should begin immediately and not await further refinement of the current federal strategy.* [p. 97]

  - As described previously in the PCAST review sections of this report, the NEHI Working Group has organized a series of public workshops in 2009 and 2010 to gather broad research community and stakeholder input on the evolving NNI EHS strategy, as part of the ongoing adaptive management approach laid out in the February 2008 NNI strategy document. One of the main objectives of these workshops is to develop a better analysis of the gaps in the existing Federal EHS investments. As discussed above, EPA has also funded the recommended BEST study to develop a broader national strategic plan.

APPENDIX A. GLOSSARY

Act	Public Law 108-153, the 21st Century Nanotechnology Research and Development Act
AF&PA	American Forest and Paper Association
AFRI	Agriculture and Food Research Initiative (USDA/NIFA)
Agencies	Departments, agencies, and commissions within the Executive Branch of U.S. Federal Government
AMRDEC	Army Aviation and Missile Research Development and Engineering Center (DOD)
ARPA-E	Advanced Research Projects–Energy (DOE)
ARRA	American Recovery and Reinvestment Act
BEST	Board on Environmental Science and Toxicology (National Academies)
BIS	Bureau of Industry and Security (DOC)
CBAN	Cooperative Board for Advancing Nanotechnology
CDC	Centers for Disease Control and Prevention
CEIN	Centers for Environmental Implications of Nanotechnology (EPA and NSF)
CNST	Center for Nanoscale Science and Technology (DOC/NIST)
CNT	Carbon nanotube
CORE	Nanotechnology Collaborative Opportunities for Research Excellence (FDA program)
CPSC	Consumer Product Safety Commission
CSREES	Cooperative State Research, Education, and Extension Service (USDA); it was replaced by the National Institute of Food and Agriculture (NIFA) in 2009
CT	Committee on Technology of the NSTC
DHS	Department of Homeland Security
DHHS	Department of Health and Human Services
DNI	Director of National Intelligence
DOC	Department of Commerce
DOD	Department of Defense
DOE	Department of Energy
DOEd	Department of Education
DOJ	Department of Justice
DOL	Department of Labor
DOS	Department of State
DOT	Department of Transportation
DOTreas	Department of the Treasury
EC	European Commission
EERE	[Office of] Energy Efficiency and Renewable Energy (DOE)
EHS	Environmental, health, and safety

EPA	Environmental Protection Agency
FDA	Food and Drug Administration (DHHS)
FHWA	Federal Highway Administration (DOT)
FOA	Funding Opportunity Announcement
FS	Forest Service (USDA)
GIN	Global Issues in Nanotechnology (NSET Subcommittee working group)
ICON	International Council on Nanotechnology
ISO	International Organization for Standardization
ITC	International Trade Commission
IWG	Interagency working group
NASA	National Aeronautics and Space Administration
NCER	National Center for Environmental Research (EPA)
NCI	National Cancer Institute (DHHS/NIH)
NCL	Nanotechnology Characterization Laboratory (DHHS/NIH/NCI)
NCLT	Center for Learning and Teaching in Nanoscale Science and Engineering (NSF)
NEHI	Nanotechnology Environmental and Health Implications Working Group of the NSET Subcommittee
NHGRI	National Human Genome Research Institute (DHHS/NIH)
NHLBI	National Heart, Lung, and Blood Institute (DHHS/NIH)
NIBIB	National Institute of Biomedical Imaging and Bioengineering (DHHS/NIH)
NIEHS	National Institute of Environmental Health Sciences (DHHS/NIH)
NIFA	National Institute of Food and Agriculture (USDA, replacing CSREES Oct. 1, 2009)
NIH	National Institutes of Health (DHHS)
NILI	Nanotechnology Innovation and Liaison with Industry Working Group of the NSET Subcommittee
NIOSH	National Institute for Occupational Safety and Health (DHHS/Centers for Disease Control and Prevention)
NIST	National Institute of Standards and Technology (DOC)
NNAP	National Nanotechnology Advisory Panel
NNCO	National Nanotechnology Coordination Office
NNI	National Nanotechnology Initiative
NNIN	National Nanotechnology Infrastructure Network (NSF program)
NPEC	Nanotechnology Public Engagement and Communication Working Group of the NSET Subcommittee
NRC	Nuclear Regulatory Commission (also National Research Council of the National Academies)
NRO	National Reconnaissance Office
NSEC	Nanoscale Science and Engineering Centers (NSF program)
NSET	Nanoscale Science, Engineering, and Technology Subcommittee of the NSTC

NSF	National Science Foundation
NSRC	Nanoscale Science Research Centers (DOE program)
NSTC	National Science and Technology Council
NTP	National Toxicology Program (DHHS)
OECD	Organisation for Economic Co-operation and Development
OMB	Office of Management and Budget (Executive Office of the President)
OSTP	Office of Science and Technology Policy (Executive Office of the President)
PCA	Program Component Area
PCAST	President's Council of Advisors on Science and Technology
RFA	Request for Applications
SBIR	Small Business Innovation Research Program
SI	System Internationale (International System of Units)
STAR	Science to Achieve Results (EPA)
STTR	Small Business Technology Transfer Research Program
USGS	U.S. Geological Survey (Department of the Interior)
USPTO	U.S. Patent and Trademark Office (DOC)
USDA	U.S. Department of Agriculture
WHO	World Health Organization
WPMN	Working Party on Manufactured Nanomaterials (under the Chemicals Committee of the OECD)
WPN	Working Party on Nanotechnology (OECD)

APPENDIX B. CONTACT LIST

OSTP

Travis M. Earles
Assistant Director for Nanotechnology
Office of Science and Technology Policy
Executive Office of the President
New Executive Office Building
Washington, DC 20502
T: 202-456-6025
F: 202-456-6021
Travis_M._Earles@ostp.eop.gov

OMB

Irene Kariampuzha
Office of Management and Budget
Executive Office of the President
725 17th St., N.W.
Washington, DC 20503
T: 202-395-3535
F: 202-395-4652
Irene_Kariampuzha@omb.eop.gov

NNCO

Dr. E. Clayton Teague
Director
National Nanotechnology
    Coordination Office
4201 Wilson Blvd.
Stafford II, Suite 405
Arlington, VA 22230
T: 703-292-4319
F: 703-292-9312
cteague@nnco.nano.gov

CPSC

Dr. Mary Ann Danello
Associate Executive Director
Directorate for Health Sciences
Consumer Product Safety Commission
4330 East-West Highway, Suite 600
Bethesda, MD 20814
T: 301-504-7237
F: 301-504-0079
mdanello@cpsc.gov

Dr. Treye Thomas
Toxicologist
Office of Hazard Identification and
    Reduction
Consumer Product Safety Commission
4330 East-West Highway, Suite 600
Bethesda, MD 20814
T: 301-504-7738
F: 301-504-0079
tthomas@cpsc.gov

DHS

Dr. Richard T. Lareau
Science and Technology Directorate
Department of Homeland Security
William J. Hughes Technical Center,
    Bldg. 315
Atlantic City International Airport, NJ
    08405
T: 609-813-2760
F: 609-383-1973
Richard.Lareau@dhs.gov

Dr. Eric J. Houser
Department of Homeland Security
Office of Research and Development
Science and Technology Directorate
1120 Vermont Ave., N.W.
Washington, DC 20005
T: 202-254-5366
eric.houser@dhs.gov

DNI

Richard D. Ridgley
Chief Scientist
Advanced Systems and Technology
    Directorate
National Reconnaissance Office
14675 Lee Road
Chantilly, VA 20151
T: 703 808-3115
F: 703 808-2646
ridgleyr@nro.mil

Susan Durham
DCI Intelligence Technology
    Innovation Center
Central Intelligence Agency
Washington, DC 20505
susaned0@ucia.gov

DOC/BIS

Kelly Gardner
Export Policy Advisor
Department of Commerce
Bureau of Industry and Security
Office of National Security and
    Technology Transfer Controls
14th St. & Constitution Ave., N.W.
Rm. 2600
Washington, DC 20230
T: 202-482-0102
F: 202-482-3345
kgardner@bis.doc.gov

DOD

Dr. Lewis Sloter
Associate Director, Materials &
    Structures
Office of the Director, Defense Research
    and Engineering
1777 N. Kent St Ste 9030
Arlington, VA 22209-2110
T: 703-588-7418
F: 703-696-2230
Lewis.Sloter@osd.mil

Dr. Mihal E. Gross
Program Officer - Functional
    Inorganic/Semiconductor/Nano
    Materials & Systems
Office of Naval Research
Naval Materials Science and
    Technology Division - Code 332
875 North Randolph St., Suite 1425
Arlington, VA 22203-1995
T: 703-696-0388
F: 703-696-0934
mihal.gross@navy.mil

Dr. Gernot S. Pomrenke
Program Manager - Optoelectronics,
    THz and Nanotechnology
AFOSR/NE
Directorate of Physics and Electronics
Air Force Office of Scientific Research
875 North Randolph Street
Suite 325, Rm. 3112
Arlington, VA 22203-1768
T: 703-696-8426
F: 703-696-8481
gernot.pomrenke@afosr.af.mil

Dr. Eric Snow
Director, Institute for Nanoscience
Code 1100
Naval Research Laboratory
Washington DC 20375
T: 202-767-3261
F: 202-767-1821
snow@bloch.nrl.navy.mil

Dr. David M. Stepp
Chief, Materials Science Division
Army Research Office
AMSRL-RO-PM (Materials Science
    Division)
P.O. Box 12211
Research Triangle Park, NC 27709
T: 919-549-4329
F: 919-549-4399
david.m.stepp@us.army.mil

DOE

Dr. Patricia M. Dehmer
Deputy Director for Science Programs
Office of Science
U.S. Department of Energy
SC-2/FORS
1000 Independence Ave., S.W.
Washington, DC 20585
T: 202-586-5430
F: 202-586-4120
Patricia.Dehmer@science.doe.gov

Dr. Altaf H. Carim
Division of Scientific User Facilities
Office of Basic Energy Sciences
U.S. Department of Energy
SC-22.3/GTN
1000 Independence Avenue, S.W.
Washington, DC 20585-1290
T: 301-903-4895
F: 301-903-1690
carim@science.doe.gov

Dr. Chien-Wei Li
Industrial Technologies Program-
    Technology Manager
U.S. Department of Energy
Room 5F-035
1000 Independence Ave, SW
Washington, DC 20585
T: 202-287-5901
chien-wei.li@ee.doe.gov

Dr. John C. Miller
Division of Chemical Sciences,
    Geosciences, and Biosciences
Office of Basic Energy Sciences
U.S. Department of Energy
SC-22.1/GTN
1000 Independence Ave., S.W.
Washington, DC 20585
T: 301-903-5806
F: 301-903-4110
John.Miller@science.doe.gov

Dr. Andrew R. Schwartz
Division of Materials Sciences and
    Engineering
Office of Basic Energy Sciences
U.S. Department of Energy
SC-22.2/GTN
1000 Independence Avenue SW
Washington, DC 20585-1290
T: (301) 903-3535
F: (301) 903-9513
andrew.schwartz@science.doe.gov

Dr. Brian Valentine
Office of Industrial Technologies
U.S. Department of Energy
Headquarters Bldg., EE-2F
1000 Independence Avenue, S.W.
Washington, D.C. 20585-0121
T: 202-586-9741
F: 202-586-9234
Brian.Valentine@ee.doe.gov

DOEd

Dr. Krishan Mathur
U.S. Department of Education
Office of Postsecondary Education
1990 K Street, N.W., #6144
Washington, DC 20006-8544
T: 202-502-7512
F: 202-502-7877
krish.mathur@ed.gov

DOJ

Joseph Heaps
Deputy Director, In-situ Thermal
    Desorption Technology
Department of Justice
National Institute of Justice
Office of Science and Technology
810 7th Street, Rm. 7206
Washington, DC 20531
T: 202-305-1554
F: 202-305-9091
Joseph.Heaps@usdoj.gov

DOL

Brad Wiggins
Business Relations Group
U.S. Department of Labor
Employment & Training
    Administration
200 Constitution Avenue, N.W.
Rm. N-4643
Washington, DC 20210
T: 202-693-3742
F: 202-693-3890
wiggins.brad@dol.gov

Linda Fowler
U.S. Department of Labor
Employment & Training
    Administration
200 Constitution Avenue, N.W.
Rm. N-4643
Washington, DC 20210
Fowler.Linda.M@dol.gov

DOS

Kenneth Hodgkins
Director
Office of Space & Advanced
    Technology
U.S. Department of State
OES/SAT, SA-23
1990 K Street NW, Suite 410
Washington, DC 20006
T: 202-663-2398
F: 202-663-2402
HodgkinsKD@state.gov

Dr. Chris Cannizzaro
Physical Science Officer
Office of Space & Advanced
    Technology
U.S. Department of State
OES/SAT, SA-23
1990 K Street NW, Suite 410
Washington, DC 20006
T: 202-663-2390
F: 202-663-2402
CannizzaroCM@state.gov

DOT

Kelly Leone
Research and Innovative Technology
    Administration
Department of Transportation
1200 New Jersey Ave., S.E.
Washington, DC 20590
T: 202-366-4334
Kelly.Leone@dot.gov

Dr. Jonathan Porter
Chief Scientist
Office of Research, Development, and
    Technology
Federal Highway Administration
U.S. Department of Transportation
Turner-Fairbank Highway Research
    Center
6300 Georgetown Pike
McLean VA 22101-2200
T: 202-493-3038
F: 202-493-3417
jonathan.porter@fhwa.dot.gov

DOTreas

Dr. John F. Bobalek
Program Manager
Office of Research and Technical
    Support
Bureau of Engraving and Printing
Rm. 201-29A
14th and C Streets, S.W.
Washington, DC 20228-0001
T: 202-874-2109
F: 202-927-7415
John.Bobalek@bep.treas.gov

EPA

Jeff Morris
Acting National Program Director for
    Nanotechnology
Office of Research and Development
Environmental Protection Agency
1200 Pennsylvania Ave., N.W.
Washington, D.C. 20460
T. 202-564-6756
F. 202-565-2494
Morris.Jeff@epa.gov

Dr. Nora F. Savage
National Center for Environmental
    Research
Office of Research and Development
Mail Code 8722F
Environmental Protection Agency
1200 Pennsylvania Avenue, N.W.
Washington, DC 20460
T: 202-343-9858
F: 202-343-0678
Savage.Nora@epamail.epa.gov

Dr. Philip Sayre
Associate Director
Risk Assessment Division
Office of Pollution Prevention and
    Toxics
Environmental Protection Agency
1200 Pennsylvania Ave., N.W.
Mail Code 7403M
Washington, DC 20460
T: 202-564-7673
F: 202-564-7450
sayre.phil@epa.gov

FDA

Dr. Jesse Goodman
Chief Scientist and Deputy
    Commissioner for Science and Public
    Health (Acting)
Office of the Chief Scientist
Food and Drug Administration
WO1 Rm. 2335
10903 New Hampshire Avenue
Silver Spring, MD 20993
T: 301-827-3340
F: 301-827-3410
jesse.goodman@fda.hhs.gov

Carlos Peña, PhD, MS
Senior Science Policy Advisor
Office of the Commissioner
FDA
5600 Fishers Lane
HF-33, Room 14B08
Rockville, MD 20857
T: 301-827-3340
F: 301-827-3042
carlos.pena@fda.hhs.gov

ITC

Elizabeth R. Nesbitt
International Trade Analyst for
    Biotechnology and Nanotechnology
Chemicals and Textiles Division
Office of Industries
International Trade Commission
500 E Street, S.W.
Washington, DC 20436
T: 202-205-3355
F: 202-205-3161
elizabeth.nesbitt@usitc.gov

NASA

Dr. Minoo N. Dastoor
Chief Technologist, Innovative
    Partnership Program Office
National Aeronautics and Space
    Administration
NASA Headquarters, Rm. 6F80
Washington DC 20546-0001
T: 202-358-4518
F: 202-358-3878
mdastoor@mail.hq.nasa.gov

Dr. Meyya Meyyappan
National Aeronautics and Space
    Administration
Ames Research Center
MS 229-3
Moffett Field, CA 94035
T: 650-604-2616
F: 650-604-5244
m.meyyappan@nasa.gov

NIH

Dr. Piotr Grodzinski
Program Director, Nanotechnology in
    Cancer
Office of Technology and Industrial
    Relations
Office of the Director
National Cancer Institute
National Institutes of Health
31 Center Drive, 10A52
Bethesda, MD 20892
T: 301-496-1550
F: 301-496-7807
grodzinp@mail.nih.gov

Dr. Lori Henderson
Program Director
National Institute of Biomedical
    Imaging and Bioengineering
National Institutes of Health
Democracy Two, Suite 200, MSC 5469
6707 Democracy Blvd.
Bethesda, MD 20892-5469
T: 301-451-4778
F: 301-480-0679
hendersonlori@mail.nih.gov

Dr. Jeffery A. Schloss
Program Director
Technology Development Coordination
National Human Genome Research
    Institute
National Institutes of Health
Suite 4076, MSC 9305
5635 Fishers Lane
Bethesda, MD 20892-9305
T: 301-496-7531
F: 301-480-2770
jeff_schloss@nih.gov

NIH/OD

Dr. Lynn Hudson
Deputy Director
Office of Science Policy & Planning
National Institutes of Health
Office of the Director
Building 1 - Shannon Bldg, Rm. 218
1 Center Drive
Bethesda, MD 20892
T: 301-496-0786
F: 301-402-0280
HudsonL1@od.nih.gov

Dr. Nancy E. Miller
Senior Science Policy Analyst
Office of Science Policy and Planning
Office of the Director
National Institutes of Health
1 Center Drive
Bldg 1, Rm. 218
Bethesda, MD 20892
T: 301-594-7742
F: 301-402-0280
MILLERN@od1tm1.od.nih.gov

NIH/FIC

George Herrfurth
Multilateral Affairs Coordinator
Division of International Relations
Fogarty International Center
National Institutes of Health
Building 31, Rm. B2C11
Bethesda, MD 20892-2220
T: 301-402-1615
F: 301-480-3414
herrfurg@mail.nih.gov

NIH/NCI

Dr. Piotr Grodzinski
Program Director, Nanotechnology in
    Cancer
Office of Technology and Industrial
    Relations
Office of the Director
National Cancer Institute
National Institutes of Health
31 Center Drive, 10A52
Bethesda, MD. 20892
T: 301-496-1550
F: 301-496-7807
grodzinp@mail.nih.gov

Dr. Scott McNeil
Director, Nanotechnology
    Characterization Laboratory
National Cancer Institute at Frederick
National Institutes of Health
P.O. Box B, Building 469
1050 Boyles Street
Frederick, MD 21702-1201
T: 301-846-6939
F: 301-846-6399
mcneils@ncifcrf.gov

NIH/NHGRI

Dr. Vivian Ota Wang
Division of Extramural Research
National Human Genome Research
    Institute
National Institutes of Health
Suite 4076, MSC 9305
5635 Fishers Lane
Bethesda, MD 20892-9305
T: 301-496-7531
F: 301-480-2770
otawangv@mail.nih.gov

NIH/NHLBI

Dr. Denis Buxton
Advanced Technologies and Surgery
    Branch, DHVD
National Heart, Lung, and Blood
    Institute
National Institutes of Health
6701 Rockledge Drive, Rm. 8216
Bethesda, MD 20817
T: 301-435-0513
F: 301-480-1454
BuxtonD@nhlbi.nih.gov

NIH/NIEHS

Dr. John R. Bucher
Associate Director
National Toxicology Program
National Institute of Environmental
    Health Sciences
National Institutes of Health
P.O. Box 12233
Research Triangle Park, NC 27709
T: 919-541-4532
F: 919-541-4225
bucher@niehs.nih.gov

Dr. Sally S. Tinkle
Senior Science Advisor to the Deputy
    Director
National Institute of Environmental
    Health Sciences
National Institutes of Health
P.O. Box 12233, MD B2-06
Durham, NC 27709
T: 919-541-0993
F: 919-541-5064
stinkle@niehs.nih.gov

NIH/NIGMS

Dr. Catherine Lewis
Director, Division of Cell Biology and
    Biophysics
National Institute of General Medical
    Sciences
National Institutes of Health
45 Center Drive, Rm. MSC 6200
Bethesda, MD 20892-6200
T: 301-594-0828
F: 301-480-2004
catherine.lewis@nih.hhs.gov

NIOSH

Dr. Charles L. Geraci, Jr.
Coordinator, Nanotechnology Research
    Center
National Institute for Occupational
    Safety and Health
4676 Columbia Parkway
Cincinnati, OH 45226
T: 513-533-8339
CGeraci@cdc.gov

Dr. Vladimir V. Murashov
Special Assistant to the Director
National Institute for Occupational
   Safety and Health
OD/NIOSH M/S-P12
395 E Street, S.W.
Suite 9200
Washington, DC 20201
T: 202-245-0668
F: 202-245-0628
vladimir.murashov@cdc.hhs.gov

NIST

Mark Bello
Public and Business Affairs Office
National Institute of Standards and
   Technology
100 Bureau Drive, Stop 1070
Gaithersburg, MD 20899-1070
T: 301-975-3776
F: 301-926-1630
mark.bello@nist.gov

Dr. Jason Boehm
Acting Director, Program Office
National Institute of Standards and
   Technology
100 Bureau Drive, Stop 1060
Gaithersburg, MD 20899-1060
T: 301-975-8678
F: 301-216-0529
jason.boehm@nist.gov

Dr. Ajit Jillavenkatesa
Program Office
National Institute of Standards and
   Technology
100 Bureau Drive, Stop 1060
Gaithersburg, MD 20899-1060
T: 301-975-8519
F: 301-216-0529
ajit.jilla@nist.gov

Dr. Debra L. Kaiser
Chief, Ceramics Division
National Institute of Standards and
   Technology
100 Bureau Drive, Stop 8520
Gaithersburg, MD 20899-8520
T: 301-975-6119
F: 301-975-5334
dkaiser@nist.gov

Dr. Robert Rudnitsky
National Institute of Standards and
   Technology
100 Bureau Drive, Stop 6200
Gaithersburg, MD 20899-6200
T: 301-975-4699
T: 301-975-8026
robert.rudnitsky@nist.gov

Dr. Lloyd J. Whitman
Deputy Director, Center for Nanoscale
   Science and Technology
National Institute of Standards and
   Technology
100 Bureau Drive, Stop 6200
Gaithersburg, MD 20899-6200
T: 301-975-8002
F: 301-975-8026
whitman@nist.gov

NRC

Rick Croteau, Deputy Director
Division of Engineering
Office of Nuclear Regulatory Research
Nuclear Regulatory Commission
Washington, DC 20555-0001
T: 301-415-7210
RXC2@nrc.gov

NSF

Dr. Mihail C. Roco
Senior Advisor for Nanotechnology
National Science Foundation
Directorate for Engineering
4201 Wilson Blvd., Suite 505
Arlington, VA 22230
T: 703-292-8301
F: 703-292-9013
mroco@nsf.gov

Dr. Parag R Chitnis
Deputy Division Director
National Science Foundation
Directorate for Biological Sciences
4201 Wilson Blvd., Suite 605N
Arlington, VA 22230
T: 703-292-8440
F: 703-292-9061
pchitnis@nsf.gov

Dr. Zakya H. Kafafi
Director, Division of Materials Research
National Science Foundation
Directorate for Mathematical and
   Physical Sciences
4201 Wilson Blvd., Suite 1065
Arlington, VA 22230
T: 703-292-8810
F: 703-292-9035
zkafafi@nsf.gov

Dr. T. James Rudd
Program Manager, SBIR/STTR
Office of Industrial Innovation
National Science Foundation
4201 Wilson Blvd., Rm. 550
Arlington, VA 22230
T: 703-292-4759
F: 703-292-9057
tjrudd@nsf.gov

USDA/NIFA

Dr. Hongda Chen
National Program Leader, Bioprocess
   Engineering/Nanotechnology
The National Institute of Food and
   Agriculture
U.S. Department of Agriculture
1400 Independence Ave., S.W.
Mail Stop 2220
Washington, DC 20250-2220
T: 202-401-6497
F: 202-401-5179
HCHEN@nifa.usda.gov

USDA/FS

Dr. Christopher D. Risbrudt
Director
Forest Products Laboratory
USDA Forest Service
One Gifford Pinchot Drive
Madison, WI 53726-2398
T: 608-231-9318
F: 608-231-9567
crisbrudt@fs.fed.us

Dr. Theodore H. Wegner
Assistant Director
Forest Products Laboratory
USDA Forest Service
One Gifford Pinchot Drive
Madison, WI 53726-2398
T: 608-231-9434
F: 608-231-9567
twegner@fs.fed.us

Dr. Robert Doudrick
Staff Director, Resource Use Science
USDA Forest Service
1400 Independence Ave., S.W.
Mailstop Code: 1114
Washington, DC 20250-1114
T: 703-605-4195
F: 703-605-5137
rdoudrick@fs.fed.us

Dr. World Nieh
National Program Leader, Forest
    Products and Utilization
USDA Forest Service
1400 Independence Ave., S.W.
Mailstop Code: 1114
Washington, DC 20250-1114
T: 703-605-4197
F: 703-605-5137
wnieh@fs.fed.us

Dr. Howard Rosen
Resource Use Science
USDA Forest Service
1400 Independence Ave., S.W.
Mailstop Code: 1114
Washington, DC 20250-1114
T: 703-605-4196
F: 703-605-5137
hrosen@fs.fed.us

USGS

Dr. Sarah Gerould
Bureau Program Coordinator,
    Contaminant Biology Program
U.S. Geological Survey
Mail Stop 301 National Center
12201 Sunrise Valley Drive
Reston, VA 20192
T: 703-648-6895
F: 703-648-4238
sgerould@usgs.gov

USPTO

Charles Eloshway
Patent Attorney
Office of International Relations
Patent and Trademark Office
P.O. Box 1450
Alexandria, VA 22313
T: 571-272-9300
F: 571-273-0123
Charles.Eloshway@uspto.gov

Bruce Kisliuk
Patent Examining Group Director
Technology Center 1600
Patent and Trademark Office
P.O. Box 1450
Alexandria, VA 22313
T: 571-272-0950
Bruce.Kisliuk@uspto.gov

Additional NNCO Staff Contacts

Marlowe Epstein
Assistant Communications Director and
    NILI Executive Secretary
National Nanotechnology
    Coordination Office
4201 Wilson Blvd.
Stafford II, Suite 405
Arlington, VA 22230
T: 703-292-7128
F: 703-292-9312
mepstein@nnco.nano.gov

Dr. Heather Evans
AAAS Fellow and GIN Executive
    Secretary
National Nanotechnology
    Coordination Office
4201 Wilson Blvd.
Stafford II, Suite 405
Arlington, VA 22230
T: 703-292-7916
F: 703-292-9312
hevans@nnco.nano.gov

Liesl Heeter
IT Director and NEHI Executive
    Secretary
National Nanotechnology
    Coordination Office
4201 Wilson Blvd.
Stafford II, Suite 405
Arlington, VA 22230
T: 703-292-4533
F: 703-292-9312
lheeter@nnco.nano.gov

Geoffrey M. Holdridge
Policy Analyst and NSET Executive
    Secretary
National Nanotechnology
    Coordination Office
4201 Wilson Blvd.
Stafford II, Suite 405
Arlington, VA 22230
T: 703-292-4532
F: 703-292-9312
gholdrid@nnco.nano.gov

Diana Petreski
Office Manager
National Nanotechnology
    Coordination Office
4201 Wilson Blvd.
Stafford II, Suite 405
Arlington, VA 22230
T: 703-292-8626
F: 703-292-9312
dpetreski@nnco.nano.gov

Ken Vest
Communications Director and NPEC
    Executive Secretary
National Nanotechnology
    Coordination Office
4201 Wilson Blvd.
Stafford II, Suite 405
Arlington, VA 22230
T: 703-292-4503
F: 703-292-9312
kvest@nnco.nano.gov